BANGLADESH

WESTVIEW PROFILES
NATIONS OF CONTEMPORARY ASIA
Mervyn A. Seldon, General Editor

Sri Lanka: An Island Republic, Tissa Fernando

†*Japan: A Postindustrial Power,* Second, Updated Edition,
Ardath W. Burks

†*Vietnam: A Nation in Revolution,* William J. Duiker

Nepal: Profile of a Himalayan Kingdom,
Leo E. Rose and John T. Scholz

Burma: A Socialist Nation of Southeast Asia, David I. Steinberg

†*The Philippines: A Singular and A Plural Place,*
David Joel Steinberg

Pakistan: A Nation in the Making, Shahid Javed Burki

Thailand: Profile of a Changing Buddhist Society, Charles F. Keyes

Also of Interest

Bangladesh: Biography of a Muslim Nation, Charles P. O'Donnell

†*Southeast Asia: Realm of Contrasts,* Third Revised Edition,
edited by Ashok K. Dutt

Agricultural Development in Bangladesh: Prospects for the Future,
E. Boyd Wennergren, Charles Antholt, and Morris D. Whitaker

Women in the Cities of Asia: Migration and Urban Adaptation, edited
by James T. Fawcett, Siew-Ean Khoo, and Peter C. Smith

†Available in hardcover and paperback.

BANGLADESH
A New Nation in an Old Setting

Craig Baxter

Westview Press / Boulder and London

Westview Profiles/Nations of Contemporary Asia

Jacket photos (clockwise from top right): Sher-i-Bangla Nagar, Dhaka; one of the narrow lanes of old Dhaka; children in a shanty area of Dhaka; a village scene in Jessore District. All photos courtesy of Rudolph von Bernuth.

Published in 1984 in the United States of America by Westview Press, Inc., 5500 Central Avenue, Boulder, Colorado 80301; Frederick A. Praeger, Publisher

Library of Congress Cataloging in Publication Data
Baxter, Craig.
  Bangladesh: a new nation in an old setting.
  (Westview profiles. Nations of contemporary Asia)
  Bibliography: p.
  Includes index.
  1. Bangladesh. I. Title. II. Series.
DS393.4.B4 1984   954.9′2   84-7383
ISBN 0-86531-630-9

Printed and bound in the United States of America

10   9   8   7   6   5   4   3   2   1

For Craig and Louise,
who saw the subcontinent as children and young adults

Contents

List of Illustrations...ix
Preface xi

1   A Delta and Its People..................................1

Ecological Setting 1
The People 6
Language...9
Notes 10

2   Hindus, Buddhists, and Muslims.........................11

The Hindu and Buddhist Periods 11
Islamic Rule 13
The Arrival of the Europeans 15
Notes 16

3   Bengal Under the British...............................17

British Consolidation and Expansion 17
The Mutiny and Crown Rule...................................19
Muslims as a Separate Nation................................22
Toward Pakistan 25
The End of British Rule 27
Notes 28

4   A Province of Pakistan............................... 29

> East Pakistani Grievances 30
> Political Steps Toward the Dissolution of Pakistan 39
> Pakistan Under Ayub (1958–1969) 43
> The Yahya Regime.. 45
> Notes 46

5   A New Nation-State 49

> The Mujib Period, 1972–1975 49
> Between Mujib and Zia................................. 58
> The Zia Regime 60
> The Sattar Interlude 67
> Ershad's Martial Law 68
> Notes 71

6   Administration: Civil and Military 73

> Civil Administrative Machinery........................ 73
> The Military and the Police 77

7   Economic and Social Development..................... 79

> The Economy 79
> Social Issues 87
> Notes 94

8   Bangladesh in the World System...................... 97

> Bangladesh at Independence............................ 97
> Regional Relationships 99
> The Islamic States 103
> The Great Powers 106
> International Organizations............................. 110
> Notes 111

9   Prospects: Hope or Despair? 113

Bibliography... 117
List of Abbreviations 121
Index... 123

Illustrations

Maps

Bangladesh xiv

Figures

5.1 Political chronology of Bangladesh 50

Photographs

Farmers transplanting rice 4

A river scene 5

One of the narrow lanes of old Dhaka. 14

The Supreme Court Building, Dhaka. 18

Children in a shanty area of Dhaka 23

The retting of jute 35

A Dhaka street scene. 54

A village scene in Jessore District 81

Village women drawing water from a well 91

Sher-i-Bangla Nagar, Dhaka. 104

Preface

The purpose of this small book is to provide the reader with a broad introduction to the People's Republic of Bangladesh—a new nation, independent only since 1971, but set in an ancient area of the world. It is a nation whose present is deeply rooted in its past. Few works concentrate on the Bengali past, and those few are often inaccessible to most readers and narrowly focused. The scarceness and narrowness of published work applies throughout the history of the area until the latter part of the British period, on which a number of excellent works are available. Good material also exists on the Pakistan period (1947–1971), but because of the shortness of time since independence, the writings on Bangladesh are limited to a small number, of which some—noted in the bibliography—are excellent.

I have had some association with the subcontinent for more than a quarter of a century and dealt directly with what is now Bangladesh on two specific occasions. The first was in 1969–1971, when the Awami League movement, which led to the division of Pakistan and the creation of Bangladesh, was reaching its peak, culminating in the 1971 civil war. During this period, I was in Washington with the Department of State, and I maintained close contact with a number of Bangladeshis, some of whom became leaders in the new country. One was Enayet Karim, who served his country well as foreign secretary until a serious heart condition resulted in his unfortunate death in office in 1974.

My second contact with Bangladesh was during 1976–1978, when I was assigned to the U.S. Embassy in Dhaka. Much of the material in this book is based on frequent conversations with officials and other Bangladeshis in a wide range of professions. I have maintained many of these relationships since my departure, and I returned to Bangladesh as a visitor after retiring from the Foreign

Service. I feel that many of my contacts would prefer that their names not be mentioned, but those who read this will recognize themselves. I would like to express my gratitude to them and to the friendly people of Bangladesh, who, almost without exception, are willing to share with an inquirer their own views and recollections. I will mention specifically my few short encounters with the late president Ziaur Rahman, which perhaps gave me a small measure of understanding of the man who did so much to galvanize his country and whose life was so needlessly cut short by an assassin.

Westview Press has been more than helpful in the production of this book. I have very much appreciated working with the editor of this series, Mervyn W. Adams Seldon, who has been a great support and a welcome adviser. Rudolph von Bernuth, the director of CARE (Cooperative for American Remittances Everywhere) in Dhaka and a fine photographer in addition to his official duties, has been particularly helpful in providing photographs of Bangladesh. It is perhaps a fitting comment on the quality of Bangladeshi public relations that someone writing on that nation must rely on a fellow expatriate for something so elementary as photographs, despite requests to the Bangladeshi embassy in Washington and ministries in Dhaka. Rudy has done a job that the Bangladeshis ought to be doing themselves.

In this country as well I have greatly benefited from conversations with most of those who are studying Bangladesh. I particularly want to thank Professor Syedur Rahman of Pennsylvania State University and my daughter, Louise, a graduate student at the same university. Both read the entire manuscript and offered many suggestions on facts and clarity. It goes without saying—although one must always say it!—that any errors are mine.

Finally, I would like to recognize the support and advice given by my son, Craig, and my daughter, Louise, throughout the many years we have spent together in the subcontinent. It has not always been easy for either of them, but the insights gained by each as a teenager in Dhaka and as a younger child in India and Pakistan will serve them well, and they have often observed things that their father overlooked. This book is dedicated to them.

Craig Baxter

BANGLADESH

Bangladesh

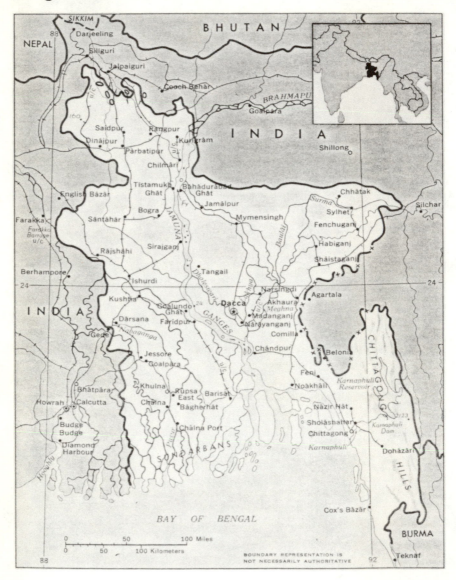

1

A Delta and Its People

On the alluvial plains at the delta of the Ganges and Brahmaputra rivers live about 150 million Bengalis, about two-thirds of them in the independent People's Republic of Bangladesh and the remainder in the Indian state of West Bengal. Not every square mile of the territory of the two political units is delta, but the delta is home to the overwhelming majority of Bengalis, whose lives are very much affected by and dependent on the Ganges, the Brahmaputra, and other rivers such as the Meghna, the Karnaphuli, and the Damodar. The ancient name of Vanga has evolved into Bangla or Bengal and, for the new state, Bangladesh, land of the Bengalis.

The story of Bangladesh covers its rivers and its people—to which we turn first—and also concerns two of the greatest cleavages of the Indo-Pakistani-Bangladeshi subcontinent: the division between Hindus and Muslims, which led to the partition of India in 1947; and the hostility between the two wings of Pakistan, which resulted in civil war, Indian intervention, and the independence of Bangladesh in 1971. An understanding of these two events is essential to the study of Bangladesh, as is a consideration of the almost two centuries of British rule. We must look at the historical and developmental periods that preceded the present nation-state. A nation cannot be separated from its past; this is eminently true of the "land of the Bengalis." We must ask: Are the Bangladeshis Bengalis first? Do they look to their shared cultural and linguistic past? Or are they Muslims first, Muslims who, even after separation, retain a community of interests with Pakistan, especially with regard to India? We shall see that they can be either, depending on the circumstances.

ECOLOGICAL SETTING

Bangladesh had a population of approximately 96 million in 1983, in an area of 55,126 square miles (about the size of Wisconsin).

1

With a density of almost 1,750 persons per square mile, Bangladesh is the most densely populated nation in the world, with the exception of city-states like Hong Kong and Singapore. To set this number in context: For the United States to be as densely populated, the entire population of the world would have to live within its borders. Land per capita is about one-third of an acre, or just over two acres per household. The annual rate of population growth in the twenty-year period between the 1961 and 1981 censuses was 2.59 percent; in the seven years from the off-schedule census of 1974 to 1981, the rate was stated to be 2.36 percent. Even at this slightly lower rate the population will double in less than thirty years; if this rate continues there will be more than 140 million Bangladeshis at the end of the century. These raw figures illustrate the most intractable problem facing Bangladesh: population growth (see Chapter 7).

Although there has been some urbanization, nine-tenths of the population of Bangladesh is rural. The capital, Dhaka (formerly spelled Dacca), is the largest city, with a metropolitan population enumerated in 1981 at about 3.5 million, including the industrial and port suburb of Narayanganj. The only other city with more than a million was the seaport Chittagong, with 1.4 million. Khulna had a population of more than 600,000, but no other city exceeded half a million. Dhaka's population more than doubled in the seven years between 1974 and 1981, while Chittagong grew by more than half. Chapter 7 discusses the many problems caused by urbanization.

Most of the land of Bangladesh is made up of alluvial soil deposited by the three main river systems: the Ganges, the Brahmaputra, and the Meghna. The Ganges rises on the southern slopes of the Himalayas in Uttar Pradesh in India, and gathers the waters of a number of tributaries both from the Himalayas in India and Nepal and from the mountains of India before entering Bangladesh just downstream from the Farakka Barrage. There are distributaries in India and many in Bangladesh, but the main flow of the river joins that of the Brahmaputra (called the Jamuna in Bangladesh) west of Dhaka. The Brahmaputra rises on the northern slopes of the Himalayas and flows through Tibet and the Indian state of Assam before crossing the border. The river formed when the Ganges and the Jamuna merge is called the Padma in Bangladesh. A third major river system, the Meghna, rises in Sylhet District of Bangladesh and joins the Padma south of Dhaka. The Indian diversion of Ganges water at Farakka has caused a major international dispute between India and Bangladesh, discussed in more detail in Chapter 8. Another river, the turbulent and unruly Tista, which flows from West Bengal into northern Bangladesh and there joins the Ganges, has also been the subject of negotiations between the two countries, resulting in a 1983 agreement on sharing its waters.

The annual flooding of the plains of these rivers is both a blessing and a curse for Bangladesh. The deposits of rich silt replenish the fertile but overworked soil, but the damage each year can also be substantial. In a typical year, about one-tenth of the land is subjected to severe flooding and at least one-half to some inundation. Levees built along the banks are seldom effective in containing the water, and the shallowness of the rivers leads to rapid expansion of the water-covered area. The force of the flood waters regularly rearranges the topography, creating new islands and bars and diverting the course of the rivers, often significantly. Building bridges across the major rivers is a risky enterprise, as the following year the bridge may well be over dry land, with the river a mile or more away. Ferry landings must be relocated frequently. Yet there are also areas with insufficient water. One of the major projects ongoing since the Pakistan period is the Ganga-Kobadak irrigation system, under construction in southwestern Bangladesh. The project is designed to provide the area with a steady flow of water, yet Indian withdrawals of water at Farakka have endangered this system during the dry season and permitted salinity to progress farther inland.

The principal crops grown on this rich soil are rice and jute, with lesser amounts of oil seeds, wheat, pulses, and vegetables. Jute is the principal cash crop. Bangladesh is the largest grower of this fiber, which is used for sacking (burlap), rope, and carpet backing. Rice is the staple food, and expanding its production has been a major goal of each government of the new state. Nonetheless, Bangladesh must import food grains each year to provide even the minimum caloric levels that now exist. In 1964, it was estimated that the average rural Bangladeshi obtained only 2,251 calories a day, of which 83 percent was carbohydrates, 7 percent fat, and only 10 percent protein. In the urban areas the figures were 1,732 calories, 76 percent carbohydrates, 13 percent fat, and 11 percent protein.[1] Although precise data are not available, it is estimated that more than 60 percent of the population eat a diet below nutritional standards.

In the higher land areas along the eastern border, which are less densely populated, there is the possibility of other crops. Tea is grown in Sylhet District, but it is considered of a quality below that grown in India and Sri Lanka. The Chittagong Hill Tracts, which border on India and Burma, are sparsely populated and could potentially be used for timber, principally teak, and perhaps some hill

PHOTO 1.1 Farmers transplanting rice in Dhaka District. (Courtesy of Rudolph von Bernuth)

crops such as coffee, cocoa, and spices. The unsettled conditions discussed in Chapter 5 limit development, as the tribes in the tracts resent the "invasion" of their territory by settlers from the lowlands. The only feasible hydroelectric site has been developed at Kaptai on the Karnaphuli River on the border between the Hill Tracts and Chittagong District.

Bangladesh has few natural resources beyond its fertile soil. Natural gas has been found in abundance and is being used to generate about 40 percent of the nation's electricity (compared with about 25 percent from Kaptai) and in the manufacture of nitrogenous fertilizers. Neither gas nor electricity is yet transmitted across the Padma, although a project to do this is being planned. Until the project is completed, the benefits of cheaper energy are limited to eastern Bangladesh. Potentially workable deposits of coal have been found in Bogra District, but their exploitation is hindered by the danger of the mines flooding during the monsoon period. Glass and cement manufacturing are other areas in which domestic resources might be used.

The river system provides a valuable means of transportation in almost all of the country, and is especially useful when road and

PHOTO 1.2 A river scene. Much of the internal commerce of Bangladesh is carried in such country boats. (Courtesy of Rudolph von Bernuth)

rail systems are interrupted by wide rivers and frequent flooding. Power, sail, and human-propelled vessels move goods and people on a labyrinthian system that often leaves safety to the whims of the weather. Chittagong, which serves as the principal seaport, is connected by rail with Dhaka and with Sylhet in the northeast. A second seaport, an anchorage at Chalna, has been built near Khulna on the Pusur River, a distributary of the Ganges.

To those living in temperate zones, the climate of Bangladesh would be described as "difficult." Except in the hill areas, there is little variance in temperature, which ranges in the nineties in the hot months of April and May, cools slightly during the monsoon, and drops into the fifties during the "cold weather" of December and January. Dhaka receives on the average about 75 inches of rain annually, three-fourths of which falls during the June to October rainy season. At Sylhet (near the hills of Meghalaya in India, site of the world's rainiest weather station, with about 500 inches annually), the average rises to about 130 inches; on the southeastern coast adjacent to Burma, Cox's Bazar receives about 140 inches.[2] In addition to regular flooding, Bangladesh is occasionally subjected to cyclones— often extremely severe—moving north out of the Bay of Bengal. In November 1970, perhaps a quarter of a million died in Patuakhali and Barisal districts in the worst of modern cyclones and tidal waves. This disaster had a profound effect on political relationships in what was then East Pakistan.

THE PEOPLE

The majority of the people of Bangladesh are Bengalis, a branch of Indo-Aryans that migrated into the eastern reaches of India after the movement of the parent group from Central Asia during the second millennium before Christ. The area was populated, probably sparsely, by Dravidian groups whose characteristics remain in the mixed Bengali population. A Mongoloid admixture is also evident in the features of some residents of Sylhet and Chittagong districts, Bengalis who are distinct from the tribal groups that remain. Bengalis tend to be shorter and darker in complexion than other Indo-Aryans who live to the west in northern India and in Pakistan.

About 85 percent of the population of Bangladesh is Muslim. Most of the remaining 15 percent are Hindu, the majority of them members of the Scheduled Castes, the former Untouchables who were designated by Gandhi as Harijans (Children of God). The majority of the upper-caste Hindus fled to India by the early 1950s or at the latest during the 1971 civil war. Hindus comprise more than 40 percent of the population in only one subdivision, Gopalganj of Faridpur District, but make up more than a quarter of the population in Dinajpur, Jessore, and Khulna districts along the border with West Bengal in India. The number of Hindus has declined markedly since the 1947 partition. They were about 18 percent of the population in 1961, but had declined to less than 14 percent in 1978.[3] There is a greater proportion of Muslims in West Bengal than of Hindus in Bangladesh.

Hindus retain the caste identification integral to their religion, and some caste associations are active in controlling members and looking after their interests, but Islam formally excludes such distinctions. Nonetheless, Muslim Bengalis often maintain a type of caste identification that can be important in family matters and in political and social mobilization. A common differentiation is between *ashraf* and *ajlaf* groups. The *ashraf* (noble) are those of hereditary high status who served in the government or the military during periods of Muslim rule from northern India and who are supposedly descendants of Arab families associated with the Prophet Muhammad. Among these, the *syed*s, alleged descendants of Muhammad through his daughter Fatima and her husband Ali, are the highest. Many of the *ashraf*, who by definition cannot be original Bengalis, used Urdu as a family and social language during the Mughal and British periods and cut themselves off from the bulk of the population, especially during the time of limited franchise voting under the British. Urdu was also used by some to distinguish themselves from Hindu Bengalis. Chapters 3 and 4 look at this more closely in discussing political development. The *ajlaf* are the bulk of Bengali Muslims who were converted to Islam in Bengal. A more modern term for the politically active among them is "vernacular elite."

Almost all of the Muslims in Bengal are Sunni; there are almost no Ithna Ashari Shi'a and but a few who follow the Ismaili (Aga Khani) branch of Shi'ism. Like most Sunni Muslims of the subcontinent, they follow the Hanafi school of Islamic law. Islam in Bangladesh tends to be a personal matter, not a system to be imposed on others who may have their own ideas on what constitutes "proper" Muslim behavior. As a result, there has so far been no strong movement toward an Islamic system of government as has been evident in many other Muslim nations, including Pakistan, of which Bangladesh was once a part. The concept of secularism in government, which was part of the political philosophy of Sheikh Mujibur Rahman, continues to receive support from the intelligentsia.

Folk Islam in Bengal includes a number of beliefs and practices that are not in strict accord with the Quran and Sharia but are common in Islam, especially in India. The local mullah more often than not will be untrained beyond the rudiments of Islam and the three Rs. He likely will be a person of some importance in his local area, and his advice will be sought in time of trouble. There is no formal Sharia court system in Bangladesh, but locally prominent persons may act informally as qadis on matters of Islamic law that are not carried to the British-inherited court system. The popularity of Sufism reflects the conversion of Bengalis by Sufi orders and the syncretistic nature of Sufism, which accords with many inherent South Asian religious ideas. Among the most popular orders is the Chishtiya, which was founded in Ajmer, India. Pirs or Murshids (lineal descendants of Sufi leaders famed for their role in conversion) are revered in their local areas, and some have become moderately prominent in politics. Most important nineteenth-century Muslim reformist or revivalist movements in India originated in the north, but Bengal did contribute the orthodox Faraizi movement, founded by Shariatullah of Faridpur in the mid-nineteenth century, which has many adherents today.

A group of Muslims that must be mentioned separately are the Biharis. The name is derived from their Indian province of origin, Bihar. Most northern Indian, Urdu-speaking Muslims who migrated to Pakistan in 1947 moved into West Pakistan, but a few fled toward East Pakistan. They retained their Urdu language and the customs of their home area, and few integrated with the Bengalis. In 1971, they numbered about 600,000. The Biharis have remained strongly devoted to the concept that Hindus and Muslims are separate nations and that the one Muslim nation should be united in Pakistan. This led most of them to support the Pakistani military action against East Pakistan in 1971, earning them the hatred of the Bangladeshis. They had earlier worked in factories and were disliked by Bengalis for holding coveted jobs. Since 1971, some have been moved to Pakistan at their request, a few have integrated into Bengali society, and some are in camps awaiting the transfer to Pakistan they desire. The story is a sad one that has received much attention in the world press.

The few hundred thousand Christians in Bangladesh worship without hindrance. Proselytizing is officially permitted but often opposed by both government officials and the Muslim population. Christian missions have contributed much to the educational, medical, and social infrastructure of the country, but there are occasional efforts by some Muslims to expel missionaries. One major case in 1977, brought by lower-level officials, was blocked by then Home Minister Mustafizur Rahman.

The tribal groups in Bangladesh may be Buddhist, Christian, or animist. The lowland tribes, such as the Garos in Mymensingh District and the Santhals in the tea plantations of Sylhet District, are few in number and have settled without incident. Of greater concern to the central government are the tribes in the Chittagong Hill Tracts. These tribal groups are mainly Buddhist and include Chakmas, Maghs, and Tripuras (who are Hindu) whose territories spill across the borders into India or Burma. They inhabit the most sparsely populated area of the country, using land that is coveted by many who dwell in the crowded plains.

LANGUAGE

Bangladesh is unique among the countries of South Asia in that it is unilingual: All Bangladeshis, save for the few Biharis and some tribes, have Bengali as their mother tongue. As we shall see in Chapter 4, the failure of Pakistanis to give Bengali a coequal status with Urdu as the national language of Pakistan was a key grievance leading to the civil war and secession of 1971. Postindependence linguistic nationalism ran rampant for a short time during the Mujib period, but a greater balance based on the recognition that English as an international language is a key to Bangladeshi development has greatly tempered this.

Bengali is the most easterly of the Indo-European languages derived from Sanskrit. It evolved through Prakrit and, to an extent resulting from the Buddhist influence, Pali. It is written in a modified Devanagari or Sanskritic script, unlike Urdu, which uses an Arabic script barely adequate for the Indo-European sounds both languages have. To the Sanskritic base have been added words of Arabic, Persian, and English origin.

The Bengali language has a major literary tradition, mostly composed by Hindus but honored by both Muslims and Hindus. Hindu hymns of praise to Krishna and other gods and the Hindu nationalist writing of artists such as Bankim Chandra Chatterjee are unlikely to find receptive eyes and ears in Bangladesh, but the mystical Sufi literature of the medieval period is welcome. At the beginning of the nineteenth century, the work of the missionary William Carey and the Hindu reformer Raja Ram Mohan Roy ushered in a new period of Bengali literature, which culminated in the work of Sir

Rabindranath Tagore, a Nobel laureate in 1913. Ill-advised attempts to stifle Tagore's works by the Pakistani government after independence in 1947 added fuel to the fire burning for a continuation of the Bengali heritage. We will return to this topic after surveying the early history of the area now called Bangladesh.

NOTES

1. B.L.C. Johnson, *Bangladesh*, 2d ed. (Totowa, N.J.: Barnes and Noble, 1982), p. 10.

2. Ibid., p. 27.

3. At this writing, the full results of the 1981 census were not yet available. The data on Hindus are therefore derived from voting data made available to M. Rashiduzzaman and me by the Election Commission for the 1978 presidential election. These showed that 13.48 percent of those registered (registration is compulsory and is done by the government) were Hindus. We used this as a surrogate in our article "Bangladesh Votes—1978 and 1979," *Asian Survey* 21, 4 (April 1981): 485–500.

2

Hindus, Buddhists, and Muslims

A look at the Hindu and Buddhist background of Bangladesh is essential for an understanding of the country. This mixed religious heritage was derided by West Pakistanis who saw themselves as "purer" Muslims, adding to the irritation of the East Pakistanis at apparently being considered second-class members of the Islamic nation. A sharp expression of this view by the West Pakistanis came after the 1970 election, in which the Bengalis voted overwhelmingly for the Awami League, as, presumably, did almost all voting Hindus. A Punjabi newspaper editor maintained that the Awami League was a party of Hindus and of those whose Islam was more Hindu than Muslim.

THE HINDU AND BUDDHIST PERIODS

The Oxford History of India states flatly: "No definite affirmation of any kind can be made about specific events in . . . Bengal before 300 B.C."[1] Most of the historical information available pertains primarily to the Indus and upper Ganges valleys, the latter as far downstream as Bihar. Bihar became a major center, and often dominated the area known as Vanga in the post-Vedic period. It is thought that the Indo-Aryan movement into Bengal may have involved groups of people fleeing the various local regimes holding power in the upper Ganges basin. This movement was supposedly preceded by the migration of Dravidian groups displaced from northern India by the Indo-Aryans about 1000 B.C. Among these migrants was a tribe called the Bang, from which the name of the area is derived. The area was much smaller then, as three millennia of river flow have added considerably to the deltaic buildup into the Bay of Bengal. There are references

11

to Vanga in early Sanskritic literature, but the area plays no important role in the legendary events recorded in such works as the *Mahabharata*.

Bengal formed the eastern extremity of the great Mauryan Empire of Chandragupta (ca. 321–296 B.C.) and his grandson Ashoka (ca. 274–232 B.C.). A Mauryan inscription has been found at Pundra, in Bogra District. The western part of Bengal, now West Bengal, achieved some importance during the Maurya period as it provided the major seaport from which Indian vessels could sail to Ceylon, Burma, and Southeast Asia. The Mauryas also brought Buddhism into Bengal, and it was from Bengal that Ashoka's son carried the message of the Enlightened One to Ceylon; others carried it from Ceylon to Burma. Almost a thousand years later, a Buddhist kingdom would flourish in Bengal.

The decline of the Mauryas left Bengal very much to its own devices, and little is known of the political activities of the period of rapidly changing states that followed the decline. Pundra (or Pundravardhana) remained an important Buddhist site. The Gupta Empire of the fourth and fifth centuries A.D. exacted tribute from Bengal but generally allowed local chieftains to exercise authority as long as the tribute was paid. The delta area was organized into the Kingdom of Samatata, with its headquarters located near the present city of Chandpur in Comilla District. Samatata was also loosely drawn into the orbit of the short-lived empire of Harsha (606–647 A.D.). However, despite these occasional connections with the heartland of India—what is today Bihar and Uttar Pradesh—the area constituting present-day Bangladesh was very much a backwater as far as the main historical development of the subcontinent was concerned. This situation did not change significantly until the rise of Calcutta as the capital under the British Empire, and the area lapsed again into obscurity when New Delhi succeeded Calcutta in 1911. One can perhaps see the historical seeds of the second-class status felt by both West Bengalis and East Pakistanis in independent India and Pakistan.

The anarchy following the fall of the empire of Harsha and its Bengali tributary Samatata was ended by the election to power of a Buddhist chieftain, Gopala, who founded the Pala dynasty around 750 A.D. The Pala dynasty ruled, with difficulty at times, until 1150. Under the Palas, Bengal reversed its usual status as tributary to the northern Indian states and expanded by military conquest into Bihar and toward the Deccan. The goal of three competing dynasties in India (the Palas, Rashtrakutas, and Gurjara-Pratiharas) was to conquer the capital of Harsha in Uttar Pradesh, and although the Palas did not achieve the goal, the former capital of the Pala kingdom for much of its reign was the city now known as Monghyr in Bihar. In Bengal, the principal seat of power was Vikramapur in Dhaka District. The Palas—so-called because the names of all the rulers ended in -pala— were ardent Buddhists who did much to spread the religion that had first been introduced to Bengal by Ashoka's agents. They founded Buddhist monasteries and schools, and Chinese pilgrims traveling to India at the time wrote of the piety and devotion of the Bengalis. Buddhism was welcomed especially by the lower castes, just as Islam was later welcomed after the reinstitution of Brahmanistic Hinduism.

The nonviolent aspect of Buddhism may have weakened the Pala dynasty to the extent that it could not withstand the uprising of a tributary group, the Senas. In the mid-eleventh century, the Senas overthrew the Palas and built a kingdom on their ashes. The Senas were orthodox Hindus and reinstated the caste system with all of its disabilities for the lower sections of society. They also introduced a version of the system peculiar to Bengal, kulinism, under which a man of higher caste may marry a woman of lower caste. Opposition to the revival of Brahmanism led members of the lower castes to embrace Islam.

ISLAMIC RULE

Although there had been earlier incursions by Muslims into Sind, the major attacks and ultimate conquest of much of the sub-continent came from Afghanistan, beginning with the raid in force of Mahmud of Ghazni in 1001. At the end of the twelfth and beginning of the thirteenth centuries, Bihar and Bengal were overrun by Muslim armies, and they remained under effective Muslim control until the British destroyed that power at the Battle of Plassey in 1757. During the six centuries of Muslim rule, the authority of the sultans and emperors from Delhi was often challenged by local Bengali governors, who sought and occasionally gained independent power for themselves.

In 1202, the last major Sena ruler was expelled from his capital at Nadia (in West Bengal) and effective control passed to the Muslims, although other Senas ruled for a short time in eastern Bengal. After loose association with the sultanate of Delhi, Bengal became independent in 1341 and asserted this with some challenges until 1541, when it came under Afghan rule. In the fifteenth century, Dhaka was established as the seat of the governors of independent rulers of Bengal and retained this position throughout most of the period of Muslim rule. The name of the city is perhaps derived from the goddess

PHOTO 2.1 One of the narrow lanes of old Dhaka. (Courtesy of Rudolph von Bernuth)

Dhakeshwari, whose temple still stands in the city. The Afghan period ended with the conquest of Dhaka by forces of the Mughal emperor Akbar in 1576, and Bengal remained a Mughal province until the decline of the Mughals in the eighteenth century.

The period of Mughal domination brought an influx of civil and military officials from outside Bengal. Many of them were given grants of land and settled permanently in the province. Although by the time of independence most of the large zamindars (landlords) were Hindu, an important group were Muslim and remained holders of substantial grants until major land reform measures were enacted after the independence of Pakistan. Many of these Muslims used Urdu rather than Bengali as their family and professional language and were politically associated with the northern Indian Muslims through the Muslim League. A few of these families were Shi'a rather than Sunni, which further separated them from the mainstream of Bengali Muslims.

In 1704, the capital was moved from Dhaka to Murshidabad. The governors in Murshidabad became practically independent rulers after the death of the last of the great Mughal emperors, Aurangzeb, in 1707. They added Bihar and Orissa to their governorship, thereby including under their rule almost all of eastern India, although they continued to pay an annual tribute to Delhi. The rulers were troubled by incursions from Hindu Marathas from the Bombay area, who were opposed to Mughal rule, but they maintained a court that could survive against the Maratha challenge. When the governor Alivardi died in 1756, he left the rule of Bengal to his grandson Sirajuddaula, who would lose Bengal to Robert Clive and the British the next year. We now turn to the European involvement in Bengal, which began long before the rule of Bengal passed to the British, who held it for 190 years.

THE ARRIVAL OF THE EUROPEANS

The British were not the first Europeans to arrive in Bengal. The Portuguese, whose stay in India began with Vasco da Gama's arrival at Calicut in 1498, soon extended their reach to the east coast of India, establishing their first Bengali settlement at Chittagong in 1517. The temporary settlement was made permanent in 1536, but it was surpassed in size and importance by a post established in 1579 at Hooghly, on the river of the same name, through a grant of land and permission to trade by Akbar. Missionary and trading activity prospered until Emperor Shahjahan drove the Portuguese out in 1632. (It was not until 1677 that the still-surviving Portuguese church at Tejgaon in Dhaka was established.)

In 1602, the Dutch arrived and set up a trading point at Chinsura on the Hooghly River, not far from the Portuguese. The British established a factory in Bengal in 1650, and founded the city of Calcutta, also on the Hooghly, in 1686. Later in the century, the Danes and the French also set up shop in Srirampur (Serampore) and Chandranagar respectively. Other than the British, only the French remained in their small enclave by the time of Indian independence in 1947. The foreign enclaves were under the control of the trading companies of each European nation but owed a nominal allegiance to the Mughals and their Bengali governors. Their initial objective was trade, but involvement in local politics was difficult to avoid. Local rivalries made it possible, indeed profitable, for the Europeans to play one side against the other and extract additional concessions. A temporary withdrawal by the British was recouped when Calcutta was fortified in 1696. Calcutta became the headquarters of the presidency (province) of Fort William in 1700.

As the power of Delhi in Bengal declined, it became more and more necessary for the British to deal with Sirajuddaula, the local ruler in Murshidabad. In 1756, the year he assumed the governorship, the young ruler inaugurated his plan to drive the foreigners from Bengali soil by attacking Calcutta. He captured the town and jailed many Britons in the infamous Black Hole. When news of this attack and of the deaths of many of those jailed reached the principal British establishment at Madras, a force was dispatched to Bengal under the command of Robert Clive. He recovered Calcutta in the first week of January 1757. Sirajuddaula, who now faced Clive, had angered Hindu moneylenders (who feared losing lucrative business) and his own relative Mir Jafar, who held a claim to his office. The "treachery" of Mir Jafar, who sided with the British and was rewarded with the governorship, is still well remembered in Bengal. The battle took place at Plassey in June. Sirajuddaula was routed, captured, and executed. As tributaries to the steadily weakening Mughal Empire or as independent rulers, the British would henceforth govern Bengal and from there extend their rule to all of India.

NOTES

1. Vincent A. Smith, *The Oxford History of India*, 3d ed. (Oxford, Eng.: Clarendon Press, 1958), p. 71.

3

Bengal Under the British

The British rule in Bengal lasted for 190 years, and developments that occurred during this period continue to have an observable impact on the politics, economy, and society of Bangladesh. During this time, the movement to separate Hindus and Muslims in India that culminated in the partition of 1947 began. The political divisions between the national and vernacular Muslim elites that contributed to the later breakup of united Pakistan also emerged. The economic and administrative patterns that continue almost unchanged in Bangladesh today originated under British rule.

BRITISH CONSOLIDATION AND EXPANSION

The first century of British rule can be seen as a time of consolidation and expansion. The second century was marked by the gradual liberalizing trend that ended with Indian and Pakistani independence. The defeat of Sirajuddaula at Plassey in 1757 and the installation of Mir Jafar (who was removed for a short time by Clive's successor but later restored) as nawab-nazim (governor under Delhi) of Bengal secured British dominance over the declining court at Murshidabad. After making one last unsuccessful attempt to displace the British, in 1765 the Mughal emperor granted the diwani (the right to collect and expend revenues) of Bengal, Bihar, and Orissa to the British in perpetuity, in return for an annual tribute. With this, Calcutta superseded both Madras and Bombay as the principal seat of British endeavors in India, and the governor, Warren Hastings, was designated governor general. Although the status of Calcutta brought Bengal to the center of the empire that the British were building, the benefits of this did not spill over into the area that is now Bangladesh, which became the mofussil (hinterland) of the growing administrative, commercial, manufacturing, and intellectual center. Eastern Bengal supplied

17

PHOTO 3.1 The Supreme Court Building, Dhaka, a structure typical of the British period. (Courtesy of Rudolph von Bernuth)

labor, food, and raw materials—especially jute—to Calcutta and served, through the waterways and later a few rail lines, as a transportation route for British military and commercial activity in Assam and in the northeast of India.

The Bengali peasantry were adversely affected by an action taken by one of Hastings's successors, the Marquess Cornwallis, who went to India some time after his defeat at Yorktown. The revenue collection system in the Mughal Empire was based on local tax collectors, zamindars, whose position was often hereditary and who in Bengal were predominantly Hindu. These officials became landowners through the Permanent Settlement of Bengal enacted by Cornwallis. This settlement not only assigned the zamindars title to the land; it also permanently set the amount of revenue to be collected, allowing profits accumulated by the zamindars to be transmitted to Calcutta. These great landed families contributed to the revival of Bengal, but with few exceptions this was a Hindu and Hindu-reformist revival. Of the few Muslims endowed with land by the action, most were non-Bengali in origin, having reached their positions through service to the Mughals. They continued to serve under the British. This group later lent its support to the national Muslim League and was opposed by the small Muslim middle class, whose nationalism was Bengali and not Indian Muslim. This was one of the threads that led to the split between the Muslim League and the Awami League. Steps were taken to relieve the peasants who became tenants of the zamindars, but the more important actions were taken after independence through tenancy and land reform acts.

Bengal served as the base from which the British expanded into the Gangetic plain and eventually to the Punjab and the Frontier. The Marquess of Wellesley, who succeeded Cornwallis, built on the latter's organization of Bengal by moving up the Ganges and by dealing with a Muslim ruler, Tipu Sultan, who was allied with the French in southern India. In the south and in the west where his armies defeated the Marathas, Wellesley was aided by his younger brother Arthur, who was to become much more famous as the Duke of Wellington. Wellesley's successors continued his pattern of expansion both through direct annexation and through a pattern of subsidiary alliances with Indian rulers. Eventually the Mughal emperor was reduced to a de facto vassal of the East India Company, although the fiction that the company had been "granted" the diwani remained.

THE MUTINY AND CROWN RULE

The British expansion was carried out largely with Indian soldiers of the Bengal Army. Several outbreaks of mutiny in Bengal and in Madras were quickly overcome by the British. In 1857, however, the British were faced with a serious revolt, called the Sepoy Mutiny by most British writers and the First War of Independence by nationalist Indian historians. The first outbreak took place in Meerut in western Uttar Pradesh, and the mutineers—many of them Muslims—drove on to capture Delhi and restore the Mughal emperor to his former status. It took bitter fighting, the assistance of Punjabis loyal to the British, and the inactivity of the Bombay and Madras armies to quell the mutiny. One result of the mutiny was the transfer of power in India from the East India Company to the British Crown.

The blame for the mutiny was placed on the Muslims. Sir Syed Ahmad Khan, who later developed the theory that the Hindus and Muslims of the subcontinent were separate nations, wrote a tract defending the Muslims.[1] Another British theory about the mutiny, which was started by the Bengal Army, would have a long-term impact on the Bengalis. The British formed the concept that there were martial and nonmartial races in India. The nonmartial included the Bengalis; the martial, the Punjabis who had stood firm with the British during the mutiny. As a result, the recruitment of Bengalis ceased except for a few in technical arms during World War II. When Pakistan became independent, the army was almost exclusively a Punjabi and Pathan preserve. The absence of Bengalis in the military, including the navy and air force, was one of the grievances of East Pakistanis against the West Pakistanis.

Changes in Government

Following the mutiny there was greater British interest in associating the Indians with the governance of their country. Some changes in social customs had been enacted before the mutiny, such as the abolition of sati, the Hindu practice of widow burning. Many of these changes were made at the urging of utilitarians and evangelicals in England, but there was also support from reformist Hindus led by Raja Ram Mohan Roy. Many Indians were already included in the administration in lower positions, and most of these were Hindus. Queen Victoria's proclamation in 1858 on assuming rule of India to the Crown stated that all subjects would be treated equally under the law and would not be discriminated against because of religion. It was not a charter of representative government, but the proclamation was the first step in a gradual process that would lead ultimately to independence in 1947. In 1876, the queen was proclaimed empress of India, and the governor general became viceroy under the Crown. The movement toward greater Indian participation can be seen not only as an often grudging concession to demands from Indian political leaders but also as a response in London to the Liberal and Labour successors to the utilitarians and evangelicals, especially the former, who believed that men should govern themselves. Not surprisingly, the Liberal and Labour parties were generally more responsive than the Conservatives to demands for home rule.

One of the first steps toward Indian participation in government was taken in 1882 by the viceroy, the Marquess of Ripon. His local government orders created district and municipal boards in which two-thirds of the members would be Indians, elected by Indians. The order was first put into effect in Bengal, considered the most advanced province of the British-governed part of India (only one princely state of consequence was located in Bengal, Cooch Behar). Ripon envisioned the development of higher-level elected bodies as Indians gained experience in government. Much of what he wished to accomplish was frustrated by local officials, but owing to Ripon's innovation, the area that is now Bangladesh has had a century of local government, however ineffective it may have been at times.

The experience gained by Indians at the local level was valuable as further elected bodies were created. With the vary narrow electorate, however, constrained by educational or property ownership qualifications, those elected were predominantly Hindu; Muslims gained comparatively little experience. The India Councils Act of 1861 had created executive and legislative councils for the viceroy. The former was entirely composed of officials and served as a cabinet. The latter, however, was to include members of the executive council supplemented by some nonofficials. During the life of the act some Indians were appointed nonofficial members. Similar councils advised the governors of Bombay and Madras. The next India Councils Act, passed in 1892 while the Marquess of Lansdowne was viceroy, did not incorporate Lansdowne's idea of election by members of district and municipal councils but did expand the nonofficial membership. The Lansdowne Act also arranged for local bodies and representative organizations that would, through an informal election, "suggest" members whom the viceroy (or governor) would then appoint. Some loyalist Muslims were appointed through this means, but the prospect of Hindu domination moved the Muslims to act independently to defend their interests.

Economic and Social Developments

During the postmutiny period there were also important changes in the economy and education. Calcutta University was founded in 1857 along with similar institutions in Bombay and Madras. The representation of Muslim students was far below the proportion of Muslims in the population, as few had either the funds or the precollege education necessary to attend the university. In the 1961 census of Pakistan, the number of university graduates recorded was lower than it had been in 1951. The explanation for this drop was that the emigration of educated Hindus from East Bengal had overtaken Pakistan's production of new graduates for that decade. Dacca College had been founded in 1842, but the city did not gain a university until 1921, and even then the majority of the students were Hindus.

Much of eastern Bengal's handicraft work, especially weaving, was performed by Muslims. The gradual development of industry in Calcutta, although it lagged behind that of Bombay in many respects, was also initially in textiles, and this, coupled with increasing imports of cloth from Great Britain, took employment opportunities away from the Muslims of eastern Bengal. The famous Dacca muslin almost ceased to be made and is now in the category of museum pieces. As jute-processing factories began to be built, they too were in the

Calcutta area rather than in eastern Bengal closer to the principal growing areas. Dhaka slipped from a capital to a district headquarters, and Chittagong became a secondary port owing to the rapid growth of shipping along the Hooghly River. The capital invested by Indians in industrial development was rarely Bengali, and the postmutiny period saw the beginning of business investment by outsiders, especially by the Marwaris from Rajasthan.

MUSLIMS AS A SEPARATE NATION

Sir Syed Ahmad Khan, who proposed the two-nation theory, had taken a number of steps to improve the place of Muslims in India. He founded the Muhammadan Anglo-Oriental College at Aligarh (now Aligarh Muslim University) in 1875 in an attempt to bring Muslims into the mainstream of India, especially in the administrative services. When the Indian National Congress was founded in 1885 with primarily Hindu membership, Sir Syed advised Muslims against joining the new movement, partly because he saw the two communities as separate nations. Not all Muslims followed his suggestion, but most did.

The Lansdowne Act and the resulting prospect of coming elections led many leading Muslim landowners to take action. In 1906, a Muslim delegation led by the spiritual leader of the Ismaili Shi'a sect, Aga Khan III, met the viceroy, the Earl of Minto, at Simla and proposed that a system of separate electorates be included in the bill being piloted by Viscount Morley, which was expected to pass in London. Under this arrangement, seats would be apportioned at the center and in the provinces among the religious communities in proportion to their numbers in the population. Only members of a particular religious community would vote to fill these separately designated seats. Thus, Muslims would represent Muslims; Hindus, Hindus; and Sikhs, Sikhs. The system of separate electorates was included in the Government of India Act of 1909 (the Morley-Minto Act) and remained the method of voting in united India until independence, and in Pakistan until the late 1950s.

In December 1906, a group of Muslim leaders met in Dhaka at the palace of the nawab of Dhaka to form a political party to represent the interests of the Muslims. Following the ideas of Sir Syed, who thought the British were the best protectors of Muslim interests, the new party proclaimed its loyalty to the Crown and added that it did not wish to act against the interests of any other community. The Muslim League thus founded was initially headed by the Aga Khan.

PHOTO 3.2 Children in a shanty area of Dhaka. The building in the background is the now decrepit palace of the nawab of Dhaka, where the Muslim League was founded in 1906. (Courtesy of Rudolph von Bernuth)

The League often worked with the Congress in its early days, frequently meeting at the same time and place, and many Muslims held membership in both. In Lucknow in 1916, the two parties agreed on a formula for separate representation, a pact negotiated for the League by the comparatively young Muhammad Ali Jinnah and for the Congress by Motilal Nehru, the father of Jawaharlal. The Government of India Act of 1919 (the Montagu-Chelmsford Act) incorporated this plan. The Muslims, however, were given a sure majority in only one province, the Punjab, and were denied this in Bengal through the addition of seats in the provincial council for Europeans and other communities and for industrial, commercial, educational, and labor representatives. Further, the act did not separate largely Muslim Sind from Bombay, thereby denying the Muslims another province in which they would have had a majority. The effect of separate electorates on the development of a sense of communal, rather than national, identity in India can easily be seen. In Bengal, the result was more detrimental to governance than in the Punjab, where a multicommunal party dominated by middle and large landlords developed. In Bengal, the system of dyarchy seldom worked because the Muslims could not gain a majority and the other non-Hindus generally remained neutral in the communal dispute. Dyarchy, introduced in the 1919 act at the provincial level, provided for Indian ministers responsible to the provincial legislatures to oversee "nation building" departments such as health, education, agriculture, and public works. Appointed executive councillors (some of them Indian) responsible to the governor would oversee the key departments of finance, revenue, and home.

Shortly before the founding of the Muslim League, Bengal was partitioned by Baron (late Marquess) Curzon, the current viceroy. He saw that Bengal, which then included Bihar and Orissa, was too large to be administered effectively. To solve the problem, he created a new province of East Bengal and Assam in 1905, leaving the remainder of Bengal with Bihar and Orissa. The new province was a Muslim-majority province but deprived Bengal proper (i.e., Calcutta) of its eastern hinterland, where many of the leading Bengali Hindus had lands and which was a source of labor and raw materials. The capital of the new province was Dhaka. Muslims were delighted with the turn of events, but the Hindus organized resistance to the partition. In addition to some terrorism, Hindus boycotted British goods, formed non–English language educational institutions, and demonstrated against the action. In 1911, King George V visited India. On December 12 at his coronation durbar (reception) in Delhi, he announced the revocation of the partition and also the move of the capital of India from Calcutta to New Delhi. Both became effective in 1912. Bengal was reunited as a province; Bihar and Orissa were joined to become a new province; and Assam was restored at a level below that of full province. Muslims in Bengal were understandably bitter about losing this chance to add a province with a clear Muslim majority to the map.

The men who would be long-time leaders—and rivals—among Bengali Muslims gained their initial experience in the provincial legislature formed under the 1919 act. The two most important of these were Khwaja Sir Nazimuddin and A. K. Fazlul Huq, whose backgrounds and careers were representative of the two Muslim groups in Bengal. Nazimuddin, a relative of the nawab of Dhaka, belonged to the Urdu-speaking elite who would associate themselves with the Muslim national elite; Fazlul Huq, a Bengali nationalist who had been trained as a lawyer, represented what would become the vernacular elite. After partition in 1947, the national elite would stand for a united Pakistan, while the vernacular elite would eventually work for autonomy and, in effect, for the independence of Bangladesh.

TOWARD PAKISTAN

One of the provisions of the 1919 act was that within ten years, the British would consider the possibility of further constitutional advance. The commission formed to do so was headed by Viscount Simon, a leading figure in the Liberal Party. The commission met with opposition in India headed by Mohandas Gandhi and the Congress but it did lead to the series of Round Table Conferences in London in the early 1930s. These led in turn to the Government of India Act of 1935. The failure of the Indians to agree on a formula for separate or joint electorates (the Congress party rejected separate electorates and the Muslim League refused to accept joint electorates without safeguards that the Congress was unwilling to concede) forced Prime Minister Ramsay Macdonald to issue an "award" in which separate electorates were retained. Under this act, the system of dyarchy would end and full parliamentary government would be introduced at the provincial level. The Muslims gained an important point in the act as Sind, a Muslim-majority area, was made a province apart from Bombay.

Elections under the 1935 act were held during the winter of 1936–1937. The Muslim League was unprepared to contest the elections fully. Jinnah had earlier "retired" from politics to practice law in London, and he returned only shortly before the poll. In Bengal,

Fazlul Huq had formed the Krishak Praja Party (KPP, the Farmers Peoples Party), which attempted to be multicommunal but was almost entirely Muslim. In the election, the KPP polled better than the Muslim League in the rural areas, especially the area that would become East Pakistan and then Bangladesh.

Fazlul Huq formed a government in Calcutta in coalition with the Muslim League. The League met in Lucknow in 1937 to consider the political situation, which saw it a winner in the elections for Muslim seats in the Muslim-minority provinces, but a loser in the Muslim-majority provinces (Bengal, the Punjab, Sind, and the North-west Frontier). With the exception of the Muslim premier of the Northwest Frontier Province who was affiliated with the Congress Party, the Muslim premiers (from Bengal, Assam, the Punjab, and Sind) supported Jinnah and the League in national matters while reserving local politics to their own organizations. The League then began a program of enlisting more Muslims into the party and opposing the actions of the Congress Party in the provinces ruled by that party. The League prepared a series of reports—partly correct, partly exaggerated, and partly fabricated—that detailed the iniquities of the Congress. Fazlul Huq was among the authors.

The increasing strength of the League and the publicity given the reports brought the League to its annual conference in Lahore in March 1940 with greatly revived enthusiasm. A resolution—often called the "Pakistan Resolution," although the word "Pakistan" does not appear in it—was proposed and passed with the support of Fazlul Huq and others from the Muslim-majority provinces. The resolution, which was poorly drafted, stated that if the conditions under which the Muslims lived in Congress provinces did not improve, the League would have to insist that India be divided into Muslim and non-Muslim areas, with independent, sovereign Muslim-majority states in northwestern and eastern India. It is important to note that the resolution called for two separate Muslim states, not a single united Pakistan. The word "Pakistan" itself excluded Bengal. It is an acronym derived from Punjab, Afghania (i.e., the Frontier, not Afghanistan), Kashmir (a princely state), Sind, and Baluchistan. Following the Lahore session there were a raft of other proposals but presumably none suggested a single state.

Fazlul Huq broke with Jinnah over the former's membership on the viceroy's war advisory council. This resulted in the League's withdrawal from the Bengal coalition in 1941, but Huq was able to stay in office by forming a ministry with non-Congress Hindus. The Congress Party had withdrawn from provincial governments in 1939 in protest against the declaration by the viceroy, the Marquess of Linlithgow, that India was at war, a decision made without consulting with the provincial governments. The absence of the Congress aided the League to some extent because for the Muslims, the League was the only game going other than the provincial parties. In 1943, Huq was unable to maintain his majority, and the Muslim League under Nazimuddin formed a ministry.

THE END OF BRITISH RULE

Following the war, new elections were held in India in the winter of 1945–1946. Jinnah made the vote a plebiscite for the Muslims on the Pakistan question. It seemed likely that the British were prepared to leave India, and Pakistan was the bargaining chip that Jinnah wanted confirmed. The election in Bengal for the Muslim seats gave an overwhelming victory to the Muslim League and a crushing defeat to the KPP, although Fazlul Huq himself held his seat. Of the Muslim-majority provinces, Bengal gave the greatest support to the concept of Pakistan; 82 percent of the Muslim electorate voted for the Muslim League. Elsewhere the results were not nearly so welcome to the League: in the Frontier, the Congress Party won; in Punjab, especially those areas that would become Pakistan, the vote was slightly in favor of the League; and in Sind, the results were mixed. Husain Shaheed Suhrawardy became the League premier of Bengal in place of Nazimuddin. Suhrawardy held views representative of the Urdu elite, but he later changed his position markedly. Jinnah summoned all Muslim Leaguers elected to the central or provincial legislatures to Delhi and at that meeting it was decided, with Suhrawardy's support, to rescind the Lahore resolution provision for two states and to work for a single Muslim state called Pakistan.

The 1945 election in Great Britain brought the Labour Party, with its implied commitment to freedom for India, to power. Viscount Wavell was replaced as viceroy by Earl Mountbatten in 1947. Mountbatten soon saw that it would be impractical to transfer power to a single state and began to plan for the partition of India. In Calcutta, there was a short flurry of activity in favor of a united Bengal. Suhrawardy was a leader in this movement, earning him the undying disapproval of Jinnah. The move was doomed to failure. As partition came closer, communal violence, pandemic in India at least since the 1919 act, burst into full flame. Suhrawardy, who had been premier during the Great Calcutta Killing of August 1946 and had taken much of the blame for failing to control the violence, reversed his stand

and worked closely with Gandhi to curb violence in 1947, as was depicted, somewhat inaccurately, in the film *Gandhi*. The British partition plan stated that the Muslim-majority areas would go to Pakistan, requiring the partition of the Punjab and Bengal. This was settled by a commission. Also added to East Bengal (as the new province would be called) was the greater share of Sylhet District in Assam, as the result of a plebiscite held there.

The British period came to an end on August 15, 1947. Many of the problems that would plague Pakistan had their antecedents under British rule. The pattern of administration was established, as was eastern Bengal's status as Calcutta's hinterland.

NOTES

1. An excellent study of postmutiny British-Muslim relations is Thomas R. Metcalf, *The Aftermath of Revolt, India, 1857–1870* (Princeton, N.J.: Princeton University Press, 1964). See also Sayyid [Syed] Ahmad Khan, *An Essay on the Causes of the Indian Revolt* (Calcutta, n.p., 1860).

4

A Province of Pakistan

The people of East Bengal have achieved independence twice. The area became independent from Great Britain as a province of Pakistan on August 15, 1947, but to the majority of East Pakistanis this would not prove to be the independence they desired. For a number of reasons to be discussed in this chapter, East Pakistanis felt they had become colonials once again, this time to the Muslim state they had supported so strongly in the 1945–1946 elections. Their grievances led eventually to the dissolution of united Pakistan. Bangladesh became independent of Pakistan on December 16, 1971. It was often said, only partly tongue in cheek, that Pakistan was held together by a common belief in Islam, a mutual fear of Hindu India, and the flights of Pakistan International Airlines across the thousand-mile stretch of India separating the two wings. It was not enough. Today, both successors to united Pakistan are members of the Islamic Conference; each has major foreign policy concerns with India; and PIA flies once again from Karachi to Dhaka—as does Bangladesh Biman.

In 1947, the new Pakistani province of East Bengal was ruled by the majority Muslim League. Suhrawardy had blotted his copybook with Jinnah by espousing the united Bengal scheme and paid the penalty by being dropped from the premiership (now designated chief ministership). He was replaced by Nazimuddin, and the cabinet consisted largely of the Urdu-speaking, nationally oriented elite. Suhrawardy, although a member of both the Constituent Assembly and the provincial assembly, remained behind in Calcutta. Fazlul Huq was named advocate general of the province, temporarily neutralizing him. Both Suhrawardy and Fazlul Huq would return to politics.

EAST PAKISTANI GRIEVANCES

The euphoria of independence soon wore off, and a number of issues dividing the two wings of Pakistan came to the forefront. The vast linguistic and cultural differences present in the subcontinent were more apparent in the two wings of Pakistan than in India, where the physical unity of the country made these differences seem more gradual. The relative neglect of the Muslim areas of Bengal during the British period and earlier had given the east wing a lower share of participation in the administration, the military, and the economy than the residents of the west wing had. Foreign trade and funds for economic development became subjects of dispute, as did the constitutional arrangements for Pakistan and the level of representation for the east wing.

Language

The language issue soon led to violence in East Bengal, as the province was first named. Jinnah embraced the northern Indian Muslim's demand for the designation of Urdu as the national language of Pakistan, although he was more at home in English and his mother tongue was Gujarati. The Urdu-Hindi controversy contributed to the deteriorating relations among Hindus and Muslims of Uttar Pradesh and Bihar, and Urdu was brought to the west wing by a large number of refugees in 1947. Urdu came to the east wing with the very much smaller number of Biharis. The differences between Urdu and Bengali have already been mentioned. Although both derive from a Sanskritic ancestor, they use different scripts, and they also have different literary traditions. Most of the great writers in Bengali have been Hindus, of whom the greatest was Rabindranath Tagore. With the exception of some polemic Hindu writing, the authors are revered by both Hindus and Muslims. Many of the most noted Urdu writers have also been Hindus, and many Sikhs speak Urdu, so Urdu is not an exclusively Muslim language either. The East Bengalis, a majority in the population of Pakistan, could not accept that their language was not to be given equal status. Speakers of the languages native to West Pakistan—Punjabi, Sindhi, Pushtu, and Baluchi, were also unhappy that their languages would be relegated to a second-class level.

Jinnah visited East Bengal only once after independence and before his death in September 1948. It was a trip he might well not have taken. In his principal public address in March 1948, he said:

"Let me make it very clear to you that the state language of Pakistan is going to be Urdu and no other language. Anyone who tries to mislead you is really the enemy of Pakistan. Without one state language, no nation can remain solidly together and function." His views, which were supported by Chief Minister Nazimuddin, were rejected by the majority of East Bengalis.

The language issue was debated in the Constituent Assembly in Karachi, but agitation against the Urdu proposal simmered in East Bengal. Nazimuddin left Dhaka to become governor general upon the death of Jinnah. He was replaced by Nurul Amin, who also appeared to support Urdu as the national language, although perhaps less ardently. The unrest broke into open flame through a demonstration in Dhaka on February 22, 1952. Students and others marched through the streets demanding equal status for Bengali. The police fired on the marchers, killing several students. The date is remembered annually and a monument, the Shahid Minar (martyrs' monument), has been erected on the spot where the students were killed.

The event affected the debate in the Constituent Assembly, which was laboring slowly toward a constitution for Pakistan. The anger of the Bengalis eventually had an effect on the language section of the document. The assembly decided in September 1954 that "Urdu and Bengali and such other languages as may be declared" shall be "the official languages of the Republic." The use of English would also be permitted for as long as necessary. The language problem was thus resolved, but other grievances remained.

Disparity in Government

The initial government of Pakistan was dominated by refugees (*muhajir*s) from India, supplemented by a few West Pakistanis and members of the national elite from East Bengal. Jinnah, born in Karachi but for years a resident of Bombay, assumed the role of governor general, thereby dominating the administration, and also became president of the Constituent Assembly, through which he controlled the legislature. Jinnah remained president of the Muslim League, which held a majority in the center and, through some manipulation in the Frontier, in each province. The prime minister, Liaqat Ali Khan, had been politically active in Uttar Pradesh and had also been Jinnah's trusted second-in-command for many years. The remainder of the ten-member cabinet included only two Bengalis, one a Scheduled Caste Hindu who shortly resigned and migrated to India, the other the brother of Nazimuddin, Khwaja Shahabuddin.

The death of Jinnah in September 1948 shifted power from the governor general's office to that of Prime Minister Liaqat. Nazimuddin became governor general, but he did not assume either of the other two offices Jinnah had held. When Liaqat was assassinated in Rawalpindi in October 1951, Nazimuddin stepped down from the governor generalship to become prime minister with the backing of the Muslim League. Finance Minister Ghulam Muhammad was chosen as the new governor general. He was a former civil servant who had been included in the cabinet because of his presumed financial expertise. The new minister of finance was an active career civil servant, Chaudhury Muhammad Ali. Muhammad Ali Bogra, a member of the Urdu elite of Bengal, became ambassador to the United States. The British commander-in-chief of the Pakistan Army was replaced by General Muhammad Ayub Khan. A last change to be noted here was the inclusion of General Iskander Mirza in the cabinet. Mirza was a member of the Murshidabad family of Sirajuddaula and Mir Jafar but had spent his career mainly in the Frontier as a military and political officer, having had the distinction of being the first Indian graduate of Sandhurst. Each of the dramatis personae listed here played a role in the fall of united Pakistan.

Neither the Bengalis nor the West Pakistanis had played a role in the political administration and civil service of India proportional to their strength in the population. At independence each Indian member of the Indian Civil Service (ICS) was given a choice as to which of the two new countries he would serve. Indians outnumbered the British throughout the service, although not many had reached the highest ranks. Most were Hindu or Sikh, and almost all of these chose to work in India. The Muslim members were very largely from the Punjab or from northern India, and some of the latter also chose to serve India rather than migrating. There were only three Bengali Muslims in the ICS; some Muslims in the Bengal cadre were from outside the province.

Pakistan as a whole thus had a severe shortage of trained administrative personnel, and East Bengal had almost no personnel. Pakistan partly solved the problem by asking some British officers to remain on contract; many stayed until the late 1960s. To staff positions in East Bengal, Britons, refugees, and West Pakistanis (usually Punjabis) were used. These men were not conversant with the customs and language of the east wing and were seen as outside masters. A number of officers from the Bengal provincial civil service were also selectively promoted to the Civil Service of Pakistan (CSP). At the highest administrative level, that of governor, which in British times

had generally been held by a member of the ICS, no Bengali held
office until the appointment of Fazlul Huq in 1954. Bengali complaints
were addressed by changes in the composition through a quota system
in the examinations for the new CSP, and also through the promotion
of Muslim members of the former Bengal Civil Service. Even as late
as 1971, few Bengalis had been promoted to the highest level—
secretary at the central government, and those who were ambassadors
in the foreign service had more often entered by direct appointment
rather than examination. The ambassadors were generally, although
not always, from the Urdu elite; some were candidates defeated in
the 1954 election. President Agha Muhammad Yahya Khan brought
several Bengalis to the center as secretaries in 1969.

Participation in the Military

The military presented an even sharper contrast between the
two wings. It will be recalled that the British had declared the Bengalis
a nonmartial race. Except in the technical branches, very few Bengalis
were in the military, although some Hindu Bengalis entered the navy
before and during World War II. Among the recruits preferred by
the British were the "Punjabi Mussalmans"; they and some from the
Frontier comprised the Pakistan Army when it was separated from
the British Indian Army. The same pattern prevailed in the navy and
air force. The military resisted changes that would draw a significant
number of officers and enlisted men from the east wing. A report
in 1956 stated that in the army only 1 of 60 officers of the rank of
brigadier or higher came from East Pakistan; the numbers were 12
in 850 for the field grade ranks of colonel, lieutenant colonel, and
major. The same report noted that less than 10 percent of the officers
in the air force and barely 1 percent of those in the navy were
Bengalis.[1] After Mujibur Rahman presented his six-point manifesto
in 1966 he is reported, perhaps apocryphally, to have said that East
Pakistan would contribute to the defense budget proportionate to its
membership in the armed forces—6 percent. At the time of Bangladeshi
independence, only two army officers had reached general rank. One
was a lieutenant general and the other a very recently promoted
major general. The leader of the rebel forces was a retired colonel,
and most of his senior officers who had left the Pakistan Army were
majors. In the air force and navy, the most senior officer was a captain.
It proved difficult to recruit Bengalis for the officer ranks and especially
the enlisted ranks, as they lacked the family military tradition that
was so important for enlistment in the west wing, for both the British
and the Pakistanis.

Uneven Economic Development

A high level of economic development was something neither wing of Pakistan could claim. Both were predominantly agricultural. The west grew food and cotton for consumers who were now in India; the east provided food and jute to Calcutta as well as manpower for the factories and the port. One principal difference was that much of the land in West Pakistan was Muslim-owned, except for the canal colonies in the Punjab, which were largely owned by Sikhs. When the Sikhs moved en masse to India, their lands provided replacement land for the agricultural Muslims from Indian Punjab. The Hindus in the west tended to be urban dwellers, workers, and proprietors in commerce, industry, and the professions, so that factories, too, became "evacuee property" as the Hindus fled to India.

In the east, thanks to Cornwallis and his settlement, much of the agricultural land was in the hands of a Calcutta-based elite, mainly Hindu but also including some Urdu-speaking Muslims. The ability of the once-prosperous farms of eastern Bengal to provide rice to the growing population of Calcutta had declined markedly in the nineteenth and early twentieth centuries, as shown most notably by the Great Bengal Famine of 1943–1944. Industry was rarely Muslim-owned, and much was in the hands of non-Bengalis, notably the Marwaris, who came originally from Rajasthan. Tenancy acts passed during the British period had improved the ability of Muslim farmers to retain and pass property rights, but actual ownership was still rare.

Muslim entrepreneurs from Calcutta and from the large community in western India at Bombay had tended to be in trade and were only making a small beginning at manufacturing at the time of independence. At Jinnah's urging, a Muslim-owned bank had been founded in Bombay. The Muslim business community in Bombay looked primarily toward Karachi when independence came. Karachi and Sind had been part of Bombay Presidency (province) until 1937, and many Muslim businesses had already established branches there. Many of this Bombay group were Ismaili Muslims (known locally as Khojas), as was Jinnah himself. To them, East Bengal seemed a very remote and probably inhospitable place. Even those Muslims who were active in the Calcutta area often were migrants from the west who saw greater prospects in investing in West Pakistan. The Ispahanis, who as their name indicates, were originally Persian, were a notable exception. They retained and expanded their investments in East Bengal while working the west wing as well. The Ispahanis had been

PHOTO 4.1 The retting of jute. Jute and its products are the largest export of Bangladesh. (Courtesy of Rudolph von Bernuth)

a major source of financing for the Muslim League in Bengal, and Jinnah rewarded them by appointing an Ispahani as ambassador to the United States. A 1960s study of major industrial and financial families in Pakistan[2] included only one native Bengali family, that of A. K. Khan of Chittagong, whose major early investments were in jute and textiles.

Investment in East Bengal was slow to begin. It came largely from Karachi-based firms whose origins were not only in Bombay but also in East Africa and Burma, where Indian investors were feeling nationalist pressure. The partition line of 1947 separated jute growers in eastern Bengal from the jute manufacturers in Calcutta. Rather than find a means to continue the trade despite the boundary— a difficult task in the early postpartition period, each country attempted to become self-sufficient, thereby expanding total production in a period when jute demand was decreasing. West Bengal diverted some land from rice to jute, and East Bengal built jute-processing factories. Financing came very much from the west wing. The largest jute factory in the world was built during the 1950s at Narayanganj, an industrial suburb of Dhaka, by the Adamjee family from West Pakistan. With the capital came non-Bengali management at all levels, excluding

Bengalis from opportunities for training and advancement. For skilled workers, many of the plants turned to the refugee Bihari community, with whom they shared Urdu. The Biharis seemed perhaps less volatile and therefore less likely to engage in labor disputes, and they brought skills with them from northern India. The most explosive of labor incidents in East Bengal occurred in 1954, when Bengali and Bihari workers clashed at the Adamjee Jute Mill.

The east wing provided the large majority of the export earnings of Pakistan through the sale of its principal commodity, jute. The very low level of manufacturing in both wings provided little means to develop exports outside the agricultural sector. Much of the west wing's cotton was used domestically to supply the early investments in textile mills, and the wheat of the Punjab was used to feed its growing population. As late as 1960, 70 percent of Pakistan's exports originated in the east wing. The decline of this share during the 1960s (due to a drop in world demand for jute) is often missed by Bangladeshis who see the early division of export earnings as justification for Mujibur Rahman's demand in 1966 that separate foreign exchange accounts be kept and that separate trade offices be opened overseas. The development of specialty manufacturing in the west wing during Ayub Khan's "Decade of Progress," the success of the green revolution in wheat, the expansion of markets for textiles, and the introduction of basmati rice as an exportable crop all combined to increase greatly the exports of the west wing, so much so that the east wing share dropped below 60 percent in the mid-1960s and below 50 percent just before the independence of Bangladesh. The complaint that the east wing was a captive market for poor-quality west wing goods was also probably not correct. Very soon after the division of the united country, residual Pakistan's exports exceeded those of the united country as residual Pakistan was able to develop Middle Eastern markets very successfully.

The use of export earnings in investment was also a matter of concern in East Pakistan. Mujib was to demand—and he was not the first to do so—that all east wing export earnings be used for east wing purchases. Because much of the east wing exports were from the private sector, which was controlled by West Pakistani firms, the firms determined how the money would be spent. Most was used for investments in West Pakistan, as these appeared more fruitful than prospective investment in the east. Related to this was investment in the public sector. To a major degree, public sector figures have been distorted by the massive foreign assistance given for the huge Indus basin development in the west.

During the Ayub period (1958–1969), two key government-controlled investment groups were set up, the Industrial Development Bank of Pakistan (IDBP) and the Pakistan Industrial and Commercial Investment Corporation (PICIC). PICIC split later into two separate bodies, one for each wing. In the first few years, the investments of IDBP were largely in East Pakistan, although often with West Pakistan–based companies. After a change to a West Pakistani majority share in the mid-1960s, the trend reversed again, and the share was about even at the end of Ayub's rule. PICIC, which was to start new ventures that would then be sold off to private investors, rarely placed as much as one-quarter of its money in the east wing. The lack of new venture opportunities in the east wing, given the limited resources for industrial development there, may be an explanation, but it was not satisfactory to the Bengalis.

The Farakka Barrage

The partition of India and Pakistan also divided the planning area for the waters of the Ganges River, as the line passed near Hardinge Bridge, the major rail crossing between Calcutta and northern Bengal and Assam. A barrage across the Ganges at Farakka, just upstream from the international border, had been proposed at the beginning of the century. The purpose was to divert some water from the Ganges through a series of channels into the Hooghly River on which Calcutta lies. The water would decrease salinity and flush out the already considerable silt deposits that were decreasing the permissible draft of vessels docking at Calcutta.

The preindependence government of united Bengal took a broader view, seeing the dangers to what is now Khulna Division of Bangladesh of water shortages and potential salinization of agricultural lands. Another project on the drawing board was a plan to develop a system of canals, the Ganga-Kobadak system, that would irrigate parts of Khulna Division and would alleviate the salinization problem. However, funds for this project were not available. After independence and partition, the issue became an international one (see Chapter 8).

Constitutional Issues

A final set of Bengali grievances concerned the framing of a constitution for Pakistan. The east wing contained about 56 percent of the total population and would on a one-man, one-vote system have elected the majority of the members of parliament. West Pakistan contained four provinces (the Punjab, Sind, the Northwest Frontier, and Baluchistan) and several princely states whose status was regu-

larized shortly after independence. More than 60 percent of the west's
population lived in the Punjab. The concept of "parity" between the
wings meant that each wing would send an equal number of representatives to parliament. One complicated formula proposed that
the lower house be elected by population and the upper house have
an equal number of members from each province, with the excess
from the west wing in the upper house exactly offsetting the surplus
of the east wing in the lower house. The formula included provisions
for disputes to be handled through joint sessions. The eventual formula
adopted in the 1956 constitution provided for one house with equal
membership from each wing, thus underrepresenting the east wing.
Parity in this important political matter was accepted by East Pakistan,
as the province was now named, on the understanding that parity
would also be achieved as quickly as possible in all other areas:
economic, administrative, and military. Parity was *not* achieved quickly,
of course, despite government efforts, and this compounded the
grievances of the East Pakistanis. In 1955, as a prelude to adopting
the constitution, the provinces and former states of the west wing
were combined into the single province of West Pakistan with its
capital at Lahore. For the period from 1955 to 1971 we can use the
terms East Pakistan and West Pakistan in the legal as well as the
geographic sense.

The nature of the Pakistani state was also disputed. Jinnah and
the Muslim League had worked for a state in which Muslims would
be able to frame their own destiny away from the Hindu majority
of India. Soon after the independence of Pakistan, Jinnah proclaimed
that all would be equal citizens of Pakistan and that religion would
be a personal matter. Many, however, especially among the refugee
groups, wished to see Pakistan become an Islamic state, a concept
that has not yet been defined successfully. There was significantly
greater support for an Islamic state in West Pakistan than in East
Pakistan, a trend that continued after the breakup of unified Pakistan.
The present government of Pakistan struggles toward a definition of
an Islamic state, although not without opposition; Bangladesh was
set up as a secular state. Beside the disabilities that Islamization would
cause members of non-Muslim communities, including the Hindus
of East Pakistan—almost one-fifth of the population, it would, most
proponents agreed, require that the system of separate electorates be
continued. The constitution had left the electoral question to be
considered by parliament. In a rather odd decision, it eventually was
determined that West Pakistan would vote according to separate
electorates while East Pakistan would use joint electorates. The pressure

for joint electorates came largely from the Awami League of Suhr-awardy.

The degree of autonomy between the two provinces was also debated. East Pakistan favored a high degree of autonomy, with the central government controlling little more than foreign affairs, defense, communications, and currency. These views became more pronounced in 1954, after the collapse in the east of the Muslim League, which stood for a single Muslim state. Bengalis recalled that the Lahore (or Pakistan) Resolution of 1940 had stipulated two states, and the demand for autonomy (with a weakened central government as a link) grew, based on the grievances discussed above. West Pakistani support for the Muslim League lasted longer, and even when it failed, the West Pakistanis continued to favor a strong central government. West Pakistani politicians and military leaders adopted the unitary views of the refugees of the earlier period, even if they did not widely accept the idea of an Islamic state.

POLITICAL STEPS TOWARD
THE DISSOLUTION OF PAKISTAN

The death of Jinnah in 1948 and the assassination of Liaqat in 1951 removed the "giants" of the prepartition Muslim political move-ment. Jinnah operated Pakistan on what has often been called a "viceregal" system. He retained the powers of the viceroy, enhanced in Jinnah's case by his own towering place in the Muslim League, permitted under the basic law that governed Pakistan (and India)—the 1935 Government of India Act, as modified by the 1948 India Independence Act. As prime minister, Liaqat continued this type of rule, although his power was limited somewhat by his status as lieutenant and not captain of the (Muslim League) team. The power Jinnah had held was divided among three positions: governor general, prime minister, and head of the Muslim League. Nazimuddin was governor general until Liaqat's death, when he stepped down from the governor generalship to become prime minister and Ghulam Muhammad became governor general.

Ghulam Muhammad, seeing Nazimuddin as a weak prime minister, began to assert the powers of the viceregal system with the cooperation of the CSP and the military. He dismissed Nazimuddin in 1953 and replaced him with another Bengali, Muhammad Ali Bogra, despite Nazimuddin's majority in the Constituent Assembly.

The new prime minister gained the nominal support of the Muslim League, which, as there had been no election to the Constituent

Assembly since 1946, still commanded a majority. But within the party there were sharp divisions, especially on the question of provincial representation in the new parliament to be created under the as yet unenacted constitution. The East Bengal group, which formed the largest faction in the Muslim League at this time, supported the complicated two-house formula described above. It also supported steps that would severely curtail the powers of the governor general under the 1935 Government of India Act and the powers of the president under the constitution. This faction wished to end the system whereby the prime minister and ministers served at the pleasure of the governor general rather than with the confidence of the majority of the house. An amendment to this effect, adopted in September 1954, was accompanied by another amendment binding the governor general to the advice of the cabinet. The governor general would no longer have the power to dismiss ministers, as Ghulam Muhammad had dismissed Nazimuddin the previous year. The same day the house repealed the power of the governor general to bar political figures deemed by the governor general to be guilty of misuse of office from active participation in politics.

Ghulam Muhammad brooded over these restrictions on his power for about a month and then, while Bogra was absent from the country on a trip to Washington, he declared a state of emergency and dissolved the Constituent Assembly. There were no provisions under the basic law for this, and the matter thus became subject to legal action. The Federal Court decreed under the "doctrine of necessity" that the dissolution was illegal but that subsequent acts were necessary to keep Pakistan running and were therefore legal. The Bogra cabinet was re-formed as a cabinet of "experts" that included General Muhammad Ayub Khan and General Iskander Mirza, who would preside over the end of the first parliamentary system in Pakistan.

The Constituent Assembly had clearly become unrepresentative. There had been elections in 1951 and 1953 in the west wing provinces, except Baluchistan, and although the Muslim League won in each instance, there were changes in personnel not reflected in Karachi. The vast change came in East Bengal, however, where the Muslim League was swept from office in the March 1954 election rout. The Muslim League governments that had ruled until the election were creatures of the prepartition Muslim League, which had been dominated by the Urdu-speaking elite of the landlords and the Calcutta legal and professional groups. They had been elected on a restricted franchise but now would have to face an electorate voting under universal suffrage (all adults over age twenty-one). The government displeased the vernacular elite by its position on the language issue (which would not be settled until May 1954) and by its apparent willingness to go along with the national views of the Muslim League. Pressure from home caused the East Bengali members of the Muslim League in the Constituent Assembly to seek compromises on representation as noted above. The government had attempted to alleviate the land problem by a land reform bill, but many felt this action was not enough and demanded further moves. If the election, which had been due in 1951, was held fairly, the Muslim League would seem to be in for a difficult time even with the continued use of separate electorates. Just how difficult was not foreseen.

Two men who returned to active politics in the early 1950s led their disparate parties to victory in 1954 in a coalition called the United Front. Fazlul Huq resigned as advocate general in 1953 and began to revive the opposition KPP under the new name Krishak Sramik Party (KSP, or Peasants and Workers Party—not at all leftist, however, as its name might indicate). Suhrawardy ended his Calcutta exile and formed a rival to the Muslim League that he called the Awami (People's) Muslim League. This was soon renamed Awami League, and the group admitted Hindus and other minorities. Although a member of the Urdu elite, Suhrawardy reset his sails and used the wind of anti–Muslim League feeling to reach his destination.

The original alliance between the KSP and the Awami League set Suhrawardy on a national course; Fazlul Huq cruised the Bengali waters instead. Suhrawardy chose his lieutenants carefully: They included the lawyer Ataur Rahman Khan, who would serve as chief minister, and the charismatic organizer Sheikh Mujibur Rahman, who would lead the party after Suhrawardy's death in 1963. He also brought in Maulana Abdul Hamid Khan Bhashani, a leftist agrarian leader with whom Suhrawardy would split in 1957. Suhrawardy attempted to expand the Awami League into West Pakistan, but though his personal admirers were considerable, the party as such never flourished there.

The program of the United Front was embodied in a statement of twenty-one points. It demanded provincial autonomy except in defense, foreign affairs, and currency; the recognition of Bengali as a national language; the creation of a new, directly elected constituent assembly; the ending of restrictions on trade with and travel to India; and freedom of trade in jute. These demands addressed the grievances requiring national-level attention, spelled out earlier in this chapter. Issues more directly related to Bengal included agricultural reforms, the use of Bengali as a language of instruction at all levels, and withdrawal of provisions permitting political arrests and detentions. The results of the election were stunning. The United Front won 223 of the 237 Muslim seats and had allies among some of the 72 members elected from the minorities. The Muslim League won but 10 seats, and even Chief Minister Nurul Amin was defeated.

An optimistic view would have been that East Bengal was set for a stable United Front government for the five-year term of the new provincial assembly. But within four and a half years the parliamentary experiment in Pakistan ended, and East Bengal political behavior contributed substantially to this. The United Front could not survive, although Fazlul Huq was sworn in as chief minister as planned, and in December 1954, Suhrawardy went off to Karachi to join the Bogra cabinet. The language issue was settled in May, but the achievement was marred the same month by riots over labor issues, the most violent at the Adamjee Jute Mill in Narayanganj. Ghulam Muhammad dismissed Fazlul Huq in May, and Iskander Mirza was dispatched to Dhaka as governor to rule the province without the assembly, which was suspended. Mujibur Rahman was arrested on vague charges of political corruption. With the October dissolution of the Constituent Assembly, neither the country nor the province was under parliamentary rule. During the interregnum, rivalry between the KSP and the Awami League developed. The United Front ended for all practical purposes, although the KSP continued to use the name.

New elections to the Constituent Assembly in June 1955 brought about a strange situation. The Muslim League carried the bulk of the seats in West Pakistan but was unable to govern without an alliance with either the KSP or the Awami League, both of which were committed to programs widely at variance with those of the Muslim League, which itself soon split in the west wing. Bogra fell in August and was replaced by a Muslim League–KSP coalition headed by Chaudhury Muhammad Ali, a Punjabi civil servant turned politician. Ali was joined by the redeemed Fazlul Huq. In Dhaka, Abu Husain Sarkar took office as head of a KSP ministry. The ill Ghulam Muhammad was removed as governor general in September and replaced by Iskander Mirza. On February 29, 1956, the long-awaited constitution was passed, becoming effective on March 23. It embodied the dual national language formula and parity in representation, created an Islamic republic, and set up a parliamentary system. Elections were to be held shortly.

Suhrawardy succeeded Chaudhury Muhammad Ali as prime minister in September 1956. He continued the foreign policy alignment with the West. His refusal to become involved, even verbally, in the Suez crisis of 1957 gained him some enmity and contributed to his fall in that year. The leftist Bhashani withdrew from the Awami League in 1957 to form the National Awami Party with a few members in the East Pakistan Provincial Assembly. Few though they were, they held the balance in the sharply divided body. In 1957 and 1958, governments rose and fell in Dhaka as the result both of instability in the assembly alignments and of intervention by the central government. Events culminated in September 1958 in riots on the floor of the house, during which the deputy speaker was killed. Instability also marked the governments in Karachi. On October 7, 1958, President Mirza (as he had become when the constitution entered into force) abrogated the constitution, dismissed the prime minister and the chief ministers, and instituted martial law with General Ayub as chief administrator. On October 28, Ayub exiled Mirza and became the ruler of Pakistan.

PAKISTAN UNDER AYUB (1958–1969)

The pattern that led to the eventual demand for Bangladeshi independence had been largely set during the parliamentary period. Little new emerged beyond a demand for a freely elected and responsible parliamentary system to replace the Ayub government, which was based on a presidential pattern that gave little scope to the members of the National Assembly. Ayub initiated a system of "basic democrats," who would govern locally with limited resoures and power but who would also serve as an electoral college for the presidency and for the members of the national and provincial assemblies. Ayub preferred a nonparty system, but he was soon compelled by political circumstances to give way. The parties were revived. Ayub became leader of the Pakistan Muslim League, the "king's party," which brought together many members of the Urdu-speaking elite (Shahabuddin and Bogra both joined Ayub's cabinet), the newly rich industrialists (mostly from the west, although A. K. Khan also joined the cabinet), and many village leaders who knew where their bread was buttered. In East Pakistan, the symbol of Ayub's rule was former judge Abdul Monem Khan, who became governor and chief executor of Ayub's policies. He was murdered in 1971.

The opposition in the east, whose members were under frequent pressure from Ayub—including restrictions on political activity and the threat of jail—included some members of the earlier Muslim

League. Nazimuddin became national head of the anti-Ayub and proparliamentarian Council Muslim League, which claimed direct descent from Jinnah and in the east included those of the Urdu elite who did not subscribe to the limited political freedom of the Ayub period. Nurul Amin also joined the opposition, founding the National Democratic Front. Fazlul Huq died in 1962, and the KSP was never revived as a major force. Suhrawardy was subjected, as many were, to restrictions on his political activity, but he worked to continue the Awami League until his death in December 1963, when the mantle, disputed between Ataur Rahman Khan and Sheikh Mujibur Rahman, fell to the latter. In the 1964 presidential election there was no strong East Pakistani candidate, so the coalition named the Combined Opposition Parties supported the sister of Jinnah, Fatima Jinnah. She lost, but by a smaller margin in East Pakistan than in the west wing.

Ayub proclaimed 1968 a year of celebration of a "Decade of Progress" under his rule. Pakistan had enjoyed an unprecedented high rate of growth, especially during the first years of the period. The growth was stronger in the west wing, but even in the east there was a change in per capita gross domestic product (GDP) from a slight negative rate during the parliamentary period to about 2.5 percent annual growth rate under Ayub. The growth, however, was petering out as the celebrations were planned, and this contributed to a series of demonstrations against Ayub. There were other complaints, including the unwise decision to go to war with India in 1965 over Kashmir; the agreement with the Indians at Tashkent in 1966, which some, led by former foreign minister Zulfiqar Ali Bhutto, called a sellout; allegations of corruption that touched Ayub's family; and a decline in the once robust health of the soldier-statesman.

Mujibur Rahman, already in jail for his opposition to the government, was faced with the additional charge of plotting with India to separate the east wing in a case known as the Agartala conspiracy case. Demonstrations led by Bhutto broke out in West Pakistan and spread to the east. Ayub offered a series of compromises. He promised direct elections to replace the basic democrat electoral college, a parliamentary system, and his own withdrawal from politics. He summoned a roundtable conference, and to ensure attendance he withdrew the charges against Mujib. All measures failed. On March 25, 1969, Ayub resigned the presidency to General Agha Muhammad Yahya Khan, who proclaimed martial law.

THE YAHYA REGIME

In early 1966, at a meeting of the opposition parties in Lahore following the Tashkent agreement, Mujibur Rahman had set forth the Awami League policy in a six-point statement. These points were to form the election program of the party when elections were held. They were: (1) a federal government, parliamentary in form, would be established, with free and regular elections; (2) the federal government would control only foreign affairs and defense; (3) a separate currency or separate fiscal accounts would control the movement of capital from the east to the west; (4) all power of taxation would rest at the provincial level, with the federal government subsisting on grants; (5) each federating unit would be free to enter into foreign trade agreements on its own and control its own earnings of foreign exchange; and (6) each unit would raise its own militia. The basis of these points in the twenty-one point formula of the United Front in 1954 is clear. The fourth point, on taxation, clashed directly with Yahya's concept of a new Pakistan.

Yahya stated that he considered himself a temporary leader whose task was to conduct free elections for a new constituent assembly, which would draw up a new constitution. He settled two issues by decree: (1) representation would be on the basis of population, giving East Pakistan 162 members of the 300-member assembly (169 of 313 after the indirectly elected women[3] were added); and (2) the unpopular One Unit of West Pakistan (created in 1956 as a condition for the new constitution) would be ended. Yahya also issued a legal framework order to serve as the ground rules of the new assembly. The principal points were: (1) the state would be federal; (2) Islamic principals would be paramount; (3) direct periodic elections would be held; (4) fundamental rights would be enumerated and guaranteed; (5) the judiciary would be independent; (6) maximum autonomy would be given to the provinces, "but the federal government shall also have adequate powers, including legislative, administrative and financial powers, to discharge its responsibilities in relation to external and internal affairs and to preserve the independence and territorial integrity of the country"; and (7) "it shall be insured that: (a) the peoples in all areas of Pakistan shall be enabled to participate fully . . . and (b) within a specified period, economic and all other disparities between the provinces . . . are removed."[4] The conflict between the sixth item above and Mujib's fourth point is evident.

Preparations for elections went forward without conflict. Parties campaigned openly throughout 1970 for elections scheduled originally

for October but postponed to December because of flooding in East
Pakistan. The Awami League seemed to hold the lead, an advantage
enhanced in November after East Pakistan suffered a disastrous cyclone
and tidal wave that took as many as a quarter of a million lives.
Mujib and the Awami League averred that the federal government
had not given adequate and prompt assistance and used this as a
campaign issue. In the December elections, the Awami League won
160 of 162 seats from East Pakistan. Bhutto's Pakistan Peoples Party
was successful in the west, winning 81 of 138 seats.

Yahya opened talks with both Mujib and Bhutto in an attempt
to reach agreement with the two men on the shape of a new
constitution.[5] Mujib maintained that he had a majority and would
dictate a constitution based on the Awami League's six points. Bhutto
countered that there were two majorities in Pakistan and that he led
one of them. Talks broke down in March, and on March 25, Yahya
used the military might of Pakistan to crack down on those he
described as rebels in East Pakistan. Mujib was arrested; many were
killed; and many escaped to carry on the ensuing civil war.[6] India
aided the Mukti Bahini (as the rebels were called) and intervened
directly in late November. On December 16, 1971, Dhaka fell to the
invading Indians. Bangladesh was free.

NOTES

1. Talukder Maniruzzaman, *The Politics of Development: The Case of
Pakistan, 1947–1958* (Dacca: Green Book House, 1971), p. 43, citing the
Constituent Assembly of Pakistan Debates, January 17, 1956, I:1845.

2. See Lawrence J. White, *Industrial Concentration and Economic Power
in Pakistan* (Princeton, N.J.: Princeton University Press, 1974), pp. 60–61.

3. Under both the 1970 Pakistani law for the National Assembly and
the laws covering the 1973 and 1979 elections in Bangladesh, members of
the assemblies were elected from single-member constituencies, with a plurality
needed to win. Women were eligible to contest these seats, but it was
predictable that few, if any, would win. As a partial effort to offset this,
both the Pakistani and Bangladeshi laws provided that some women members
would be elected by the directly elected members of the assembly. Under
the Pakistani law for the National Assembly in 1970, this election was held
separately for East and West Pakistan. Seven East Pakistani women were
chosen and six West Pakistani.

4. The text of the Legal Framework Order of March 30, 1970, is
contained in a number of sources, including Government of India, Ministry
of External Affairs, *Bangladesh Documents* (New Delhi, 1971), pp. 49–65. This
volume and a second volume published later (1973) contain many documents

on the 1970–1971 period, and include press commentary in addition to official documents and statements. The full texts of other documents mentioned in the text can also be found in these two volumes.

5. The negotiations among Yahya, Mujib, and Bhutto have been discussed by a number of writers. See the works by Muhith, Moudud Ahmad, Shelly, and Baxter listed in the bibliography under "Civil War and Independence." See also Craig Baxter, "Pakistan, The Failure of Political Negotiations," *Asian Survey* 12, 5 (May 1972); and Zulfikar Ali Bhutto, *The Great Tragedy* (Karachi: Pakistan People's Party, 1971).

6. For the military details of the war, see A.M.A. Muhith, *Bangladesh: Emergence of a Nation* (Dacca: Bangladesh Books International, 1978); Hasan Askari Risvi, *Internal Strife and External Intervention: India's Role in the Civil War in East Pakistan [Bangladesh]* (Lahore, Pakistan: Progressive Publishers, 1981); and Talukder Maniruzzaman, *The Bangladesh Revolution and Its Aftermath* (Dacca: Bangladesh Books International, 1980).

5

A New Nation-State

Bangladesh had become an independent state, recognized initially only by India and Bhutan. No longer would questions of national language, unequal representation in parliament and the civil and military services, disparity in economic development, or division of export earnings be matters for debate with Islamabad (the new Pakistani capital). The autonomy demands of the Awami League had been carried to their logical conclusion, although separation was not the initial preelection goal for most Awami Leaguers. Little thought had been given to what a new government would do with autonomy, much less with independence. The natural resources of Bangladesh would be no greater than those of East Pakistan, and the purported financial "drain" by West Pakistan proved to be much less than had been claimed. Many managerial skills were lost as West Pakistanis departed, and this occurred in public enterprises and government as well as in the private sector.

THE MUJIB PERIOD, 1972–1975

Despite these problems, Bangladesh could now order its form of government and its society as it wished (see Figure 5.1 for a political chronology). At independence, Sheikh Mujibur Rahman was in jail in West Pakistan, where he had been taken after his arrest on March 25. He had been tried for treason and convicted by a military court, which recommended the death penalty. Yahya did not carry out the sentence, perhaps as a result of pleas made by many foreign governments. With the surrender of Pakistani forces in Dhaka and the Indian proclamation of a cease-fire in the west, Yahya yielded power to a civilian government under Bhutto, who released Mujib and permitted him to return to Dhaka via London and New Delhi.

49

FIGURE 5.1
Political Chronology of Bangladesh

Dec. 16, 1971: Fall of Dhaka. Provisional government formed in April 1971 continues in office, headed by Abdus Samad Azad as acting president and Tajuddin Ahmad as prime minister.

Jan. 10, 1971: Sheikh Mujibur Rahman returns to Dhaka to become prime minister. Justice Abu Sayeed Chaudhury is named president.

Dec. 16, 1972: Parliamentary constitution, adopted in November, takes effect.

Mar. 7, 1972: Parliamentary elections won overwhelmingly by the Awami League headed by Mujibur Rahman.

Dec. 24, 1974: Chaudhury resigns as president. Replaced by Muhammadullah.

Dec. 28, 1974: State of emergency declared. Fundamental rights suspended.

Jan. 25, 1975: Constitution amended, ending parliamentary system and establishing presidential rule with Mujibur Rahman as president.

June 6, 1975: Constitution of new single party, Bangladesh Krishak Sramik Awami League (BAKSAL) announced with Mujibur Rahman head of only legal party in country.

Aug. 15, 1975: Mujibur Rahman assassinated in "majors' plot." Majors designate Khondakar Mushtaque Ahmad as president. In the following days, he promises new parliamentary elections and return to parliamentary system. He abolishes BAKSAL.

Nov. 3–5, 1975: Attempted coup by Brigadier Khalid Musharaf results in his death, resignation of Mushtaque Ahmad, installation of A.S.M. Sayem as president and chief martial law administrator (CMLA). Rise of Major General Ziaur Rahman as leading figure.

Nov. 30, 1976: Ziaur Rahman becomes CMLA. Sayem remains president.

Apr. 21, 1977: Sayem resigns as president on grounds of "ill health." Ziaur Rahman becomes president.

May 30, 1977: Ziaur Rahman wins referendum on his continuance in office as president with 98.9 percent of the votes.

June 3, 1977: Justice Abdus Sattar named vice-president.

June 3, 1978: Ziaur Rahman elected president.

Feb. 18, 1979: Parliamentary election gives Ziaur Rahman's Bangladesh Nationalist party (BNP) 207 of 300 seats. Principal faction of Awami League is second with 39 seats. Shah Azizur Rahman named prime minister.

May 30, 1981: Ziaur Rahman assassinated. Sattar becomes acting president.

Nov. 15, 1981: Sattar elected president.

Mar. 24, 1982: Coup led by Lt. Gen. H. M. Ershad ousts Sattar and his government, suspends constitution, dissolves parliament, and abolishes parties. Ershad becomes CMLA and, later, adds the title president of the council of ministers.

Mar. 27, 1982: Justice Abul Fazal Muhammad Ahsanuddin Chaudhury named president by Ershad.

Dec. 11, 1983: Chaudhury resigns as president for "personal reasons." Ershad assumes presidency.

Mar. 30, 1984: Ataur Rahman Khan appointed prime minister (he had been chief minister of East Pakistan several times between 1956 and 1958). Ershad relinquishes post of president of the council of ministers but retains presidency of nation.

May 27, 1984: Announced date for both presidential and parliamentary elections.

Mujib, the head of Bangladesh's government to be, met with British and Indian officials as well as with Bhutto before returning home.

Bangladesh had first been declared independent on March 26, 1971, on a station identifying itself as the "Voice of Independent Bangladesh." On March 28, a "Major Zia" announced the formation of a government with himself at its head. The new government operated from a radio station in Chittagong that Zia and his troops controlled; "Major Zia" was, of course, the future Major General Ziaur Rahman, president of Bangladesh, who was as yet unknown to Western sources. It is said that Mujib's less-than-favorable treatment of Zia, who was a genuine hero of the resistance (Mujib refused to name him chief of staff of the army), was a result of Zia's claiming head-of-state status for himself rather than in Mujib's name.

More practically, a number of leading Awami League members who were able to escape from East Pakistan formed a "provisional" government in Calcutta on April 12 and issued a proclamation of independence at Mujibnagar on April 17, effective retroactively from April 10. Mujib was named president, but in his absence Syed Nazrul Islam, the vice-president, became acting president. Tajuddin Ahmad was named prime minister, and Khondakar Mushtaque Ahmad, later a president, was a member of the cabinet. Colonel M.A.G. Osmany, a retired Pakistan Army officer, was appointed commander-in-chief of the Mukti Bahini, the rebel force, with Zia as one of the sector commanders. On December 6, India became the first country to recognize the new regime.

During the summer of 1971, a number of Bengali officers of the Pakistan Foreign Service defected and were permitted to remain in the countries they were serving in. Much of this was coordinated by Justice Abu Sayeed Chaudhury, who was, ironically, representing Pakistan in Geneva at a human rights conference when the military crackdown took place. Chaudhury became president of Bangladesh after independence. Some civil servants were also able to cross the border to India to join the exile government in Calcutta. Many Bengali military officers and enlisted men joined the Mukti Bahini, which was also augmented by new enlistees, many from the colleges. At first India provided sanctuary, supplies, and training; in November, the Indian military intervened directly.

Some organization was thus in place when the West Pakistani surrender came. A jarring note still recalled by Bangladeshis was that no representative of the Bangladeshi government-in-exile or of the Mukti Bahini was present at the ceremony of surrender on December 16. It was not until December 22 that the government arrived in Dhaka, having been forced to heed the plea of the Indian military that order must first be restored. On January 10, 1972, Mujib arrived from London to an enthusiastic welcome. He assumed the presidency but vacated it two days later to become prime minister instead. Abu Sayeed Chaudhury became president. Bangladesh was now ready to establish itself as a new nation-state.

A New Constitution

The framing of a constitution was not a difficult task. Mujib favored a parliamentary form of government, and his abdication of the presidency in favor of the prime ministership affirmed this. The unacknowledged model for the document was India's constitution. The federal provisions of the Indian constitution were omitted, as Bangladesh would be a unitary state. The prime minister was appointed by the president, but the appointment would need to be approved by the single-house parliament, and he would choose his own ministers. Until new elections could be held, all available East Pakistani members of the National Assembly and the East Pakistan Provincial Assembly would be members of the parliament. (Both of the non–Awami League National Assembly members elected in 1970 chose to remain in Pakistan.) Elections would be held directly through universal adult suffrage, but the additional seats for women would still be elected indirectly. Electorates would be joint and not separate. The higher judiciary would be independent from the executive from the beginning, and over time the magisterial powers of district and lower officers would be removed and the judiciary at all levels would become separate. The rights of citizens would be guaranteed and enforced through the judicial system. The constitution was, therefore, what might be expected of a member of the Commonwealth drawing on the Westminster model, as partly modified by the experience of British India.

Also enshrined in the constitution were the principles on which Bangladesh would be governed. These came to be known as the tenets of Mujibism (or Mujibbad). The four pillars were nationalism, socialism, secularism, and democracy. These principles were those of the Awami League; the emphasis on secularism differed markedly from the focus of the Muslim League. The Awami League had run several successful Hindu candidates in the 1970 elections and had clearly gained the votes of most of the minorities, except for those of the Chittagong Hill Tracts. There were also two Hindu members in Mujib's new cabinet. With the obvious efforts to accommodate the minorities, the goal of nationalism was not difficult to accomplish, especially as the Bengali language was shared by almost everyone in the new nation. There were some problems. Democracy suffered as the problems increased and as the opposition to Mujib rose correspondingly; socialism ran wild and hampered economic growth. The Mujib program was nonetheless widely accepted and remains a cornerstone of present Awami League policy and, with some modification, of the parties of the center and center-left.

Devastation and Dissent

Mujib returned to a country devastated by civil war. Law and order problems would vie with rehabilitation as major concerns. How many were killed, wounded, raped, and displaced will never be known. The road and rail transportation system was severely crippled both by the Pakistanis and the Mukti Bahini, not only impeding recovery but also placing almost insurmountable barriers to food distribution, mitigated only by the availability of water routes for undamaged boats. The seaport of Chittagong required major attention to clear the harbor and make it usable for overseas rehabilitation supplies. Most, but not all, of the refugees returned, many to find that their homes and lands had been taken by others. There was a shortage of trained and competent administrators. It was not far from the mark to describe Bangladesh as an international basket case.[1]

The arming of so many persons in the struggle against the West Pakistanis put a substantial number of weapons in the hands of persons over whom the government had little control. Some belonged to bands that had not come under the full control of the government-in-exile and whose members espoused political views far to the left of the centrist Awami League. Conversely, the Pakistanis had armed some groups, Bihari and Bengali, that opposed secession. Some members of these groups were executed without the legal due process the new government had pledged to establish. Mujib called upon all persons not formally part of the Bangladesh Army, as a major segment of the Mukti Bahini became, to surrender weapons, but it was clear to any observer that this was ignored as often as not. Law-and-order problems aggravated by large numbers of arms and difficult conditions continued throughout Mujib's tenure, and helped provoke his suspension of democracy.

Organization of the Government and the Military

Mujib included in his cabinet his close associates in the preindependence struggle, drawn from all elements in the party. None had had previous ministerial experience, and most had incurred

PHOTO 5.1 A Dhaka street scene. The "cycle-rickshaw" is by far the most common means of transportation in a city almost without motorized taxis. (Courtesy of Rudolph von Bernuth)

political debts that often were met through corrupt practices. Leftists Abdus Samad Azad and Tajuddin Ahmad, who headed the foreign and finance ministries, were, at least initially, antagonistic toward the United States as a result of the "tilt" policy of Nixon and Kissinger. The right was headed by Mushtaque Ahmad, more Islamic and conservative in his views than the mainstream of the Awami League. Professionally competent but politically a novice, Kamal Husain piloted the constitution bill through parliament and in time succeeded Azad in the foreign ministry. Student and other (primarily labor) groups affiliated with the Awami League were generally more leftist than the mainstream and impatient with the progress being made. Some eventually broke with Mujib. Mujib himself was not immune from nepotism, and several of his relatives, including a nephew, Sheikh Fazlul Huq "Moni," who was killed in the coup against Mujib, obtained lucrative positions. Mujib was proving early that the charismatic leader of a preindependence movement is seldom the person who can successfully lead an independent country.

Mujib also denied himself the skills of many top-level CSP and other civil officers. Those officers who had escaped from East Pakistan, along with those who had defected overseas or escaped from posts in West Pakistan, were readily accepted. Those who had remained at their posts in East Pakistan were under a cloud of suspicion. Most were unable to return to service until after the fall of Mujib, even though some had felt in 1971 that staying on would help maintain such vital services as food distribution. Other officers were caught in West Pakistan. Some resigned their posts, others were dismissed, and some continued to work in the hope that there would be some resolution of the war. Those interned were not allowed to return until 1973, following agreements among India, Pakistan, and Bangladesh relating to detainees and prisoners of war. At best, Mujib used both those who stayed on in East Pakistan and those who were "repatriates" in the functionless posts of "officers on special duty." Many were simply unemployed. To fill the gaps there were many political appointments—a payment of debts to persons who were often unskilled, and far too frequently, also corrupt.

The organization of the military was a particularly difficult problem, one that, as events showed, was handled poorly. Three streams contributed to the military: (1) the officers and men of the Pakistani military who were able to participate in the freedom war, (2) the civilians who fought in the war and who wished to remain, and (3) the repatriates who were allowed to return from Pakistan in

1973. Mujib, understandably, depended on those from the first two categories; the second group was especially loyal to him.

The repatriates, who made up about half of the 55,000-man army in 1975, often maintained the traditions of the Pakistan Army, which were in turn based on the British background of the subcontinent. They saw the military as a highly selective and trained organization that should serve the government in power and not be expected to adulate a single individual—an ideal betrayed in the series of military coups. The repatriates often were denied posts their seniority entitled them to; this was partly the result of rapid promotions of freedom fighters as Bangladesh created its own forces. At the other extreme, some freedom fighters, including a few who had served in the army, envisioned a "people's army" that would even elect officers. This element was soon weeded out; some became associated with the Jatiyo Samajtantrik Party (JSD, the National Socialist Party). Mujib also created a personal army, the Jatiyo Rakhi Bahini (Security Force), whose 10,000-odd members took an oath to Mujib and were given preference in privileges and supplies. Discontent over this contributed greatly to the military action that ended the Mujib era in 1975.

The burden placed on the government by the large-scale nationalization of Bangladeshi manufacturing and trading enterprises and the takeover of West Pakistani property added to the difficulties of the administrative services. Until the division of the assets and liabilities of united Pakistan was settled, all West Pakistani properties were nationalized. Banks, insurance companies, and other financial institutions were taken over by the government. International trading in commodities was similarly nationalized, as was the property of many Bangladeshis in the private sector. These firms were usually brought together in sectoral combines managed by persons with little, if any, experience. The result was to turn often profitable enterprises into drains on the public funds. The very small pool of Bangladeshi entrepreneurs was choked off, and many emigrated.

The enforced use of Bengali at all levels of government and education produced mixed results. It did give a larger number of people access to the government, which formerly had frequently used English. It meant no practical change for the lower levels of education except for the well-to-do, who were accustomed to sending their children to English-language schools. However, it hurt Bangladesh's chances of participating in technical and other knowledge at the university level, where English had generally been the medium of instruction. Access to books and articles in that international language was now strictly curtailed.

The government also banned the Muslim League (all three branches) and other parties that were assumed to have favored united Pakistan or that had an Islamic bias. It probably made but little difference in the 1973 election, as the euphoria for Mujib (Bangabandhu, the "friend of Bengal") and the Awami League was still high. The Awami League won 73.2 percent of the vote and 292 of 300 directly elected seats (307 of 315 when the indirectly elected women were added). The election was blatantly and quite unnecessarily rigged by the Awami League, with the support of many in the government. The "pro-Moscow" faction of the National Awami Party polled just over 8 percent of the vote; the Bhashani-led "pro-Peking" faction won a bit more than 5 percent. A newcomer on the scene was the JSD, which drew 6.5 percent. The JSD was composed largely of one-time Awami Leaguers (and some ex-military men, as noted above) who thought the "bourgeois" mainstream was too slow in adopting socialist measures to speed the reconstruction and development of the country. The JSD has never fared well in elections, but at times its influence has been greater than its election support.

Breakdown of Democracy

After the election, the economic and security situation began to deteriorate rapidly, and Mujib's popularity, shaken by what some viewed as too close an alliance with India, declined as well. Mujib had displayed a paternalistic and authoritarian personality; his constant references to "my country" and "my people" were wearing thin. Widespread flooding and the ensuing famine created severe hardship conditions, which were aggravated by growing law-and-order problems. The targets of attack were often Awami Leaguers, because of rural corruption and because they represented the government party. In December 1974, Mujib declared a state of emergency, giving him personal power to order arrests and to limit the independence of the judiciary and the freedom of the press. The last was a prelude to nationalizing the newspaper with the highest circulation, *Ittefaq*, and one other important paper. Two newspapers had already fallen into government hands as evacuee property. Only these were allowed to publish.

In January 1975, the constitution was amended to make Mujib (by name) president for five years and to give him full executive powers. He was also authorized to form a single party, which he did in June. He christened the new group the Bangladesh Krishak Sramik Awami League (BAKSAL, Bangladesh Peasants, Workers, and Peoples League) drawing on the name of Fazlul Huq's KSP. This is an interesting point, as much of Mujib's political behavior in a democratic setting was drawn from the vernacular elite pattern of Fazlul Huq rather than from the aristocratic Calcutta background of Suhrawardy. Opposition parties were banned, although some of the leftist parties merged with BAKSAL. Party membership was required of civil servants, politicizing the neutral position of that segment. Court enforcement of the fundamental rights enumerated in the constitution ceased. A fledgling democratic regime had been transformed into a personal dictatorship led by a person whose competence as a government leader was demonstrably inadequate.

On the morning of August 15, 1975, Mujib and several members of his family were murdered in a coup engineered by a group of army officers, mostly majors, some of whom Mujib had dropped from the army almost a year earlier. They represented the grievances of the military, including their subordination to the Rakhi Bahini and Mujib's political intervention to save party allies and family members arrested in antismuggling campaigns. Few in Dhaka lamented the death of Mujib, so low had his popularity fallen. Perhaps the greatest expression of regret came from Indian prime minister Indira Gandhi, who had lost an ally.

BETWEEN MUJIB AND ZIA

The majors arrested three senior members of Mujib's cabinet, who joined former minister Tajuddin Ahmad and many others close to Mujib in Dhaka Central Jail. This brought Khondakar Mushtaque Ahmad to the head of the cabinet list, and the majors selected him to be president. He claimed to have had no advance knowledge about the coup, and although many Awami Leaguers doubt this, no evidence has been produced to contradict him. Mushtaque was seen as a more conservative member of the Awami League, leaning toward the West, less pleased with the Indian tie, and more Islamic in his socioreligious views. He gained immediate recognition from Pakistan, and Saudi Arabia and the People's Republic of China also established diplomatic relations very quickly. Ten of the eighteen ministers in Mujib's cabinet remained with Mushtaque. He announced in October that the parliamentary system would be restored, that political activity would begin in August 1976, and that a general election would be held in February 1977. In the interim, political parties would be banned, and the constitutional provision for a single party would be repealed, disbanding BAKSAL. However, Mushtaque remained under the influence of the majors, who moved into the presidential residence with him. Major General Ziaur Rahman was made chief of staff of the army, a position Mujib had denied him.

There was discontent in the army against the majors, especially on the part of officers loyal to Mujib. At a minimum, they believed that the relatively junior majors should not be involved in governing; at the maximum, some felt the majors should be punished for the murders they had committed or instigated. The leader of these discontented officers was Brigadier Khalid Musharaf, like Zia a freedom fighter. Musharaf led a coup on November 3, 1975, touching off a confusion that lasted several days. Mushtaque permitted the majors to escape from Dhaka to Bangkok but was himself forced to resign the presidency in favor of Chief Justice A.S.M. Sayem. Musharaf promoted himself to major general and replaced Army Chief of Staff Zia, who was placed under house arrest. Musharaf's wife and mother then joined a procession to Mujib's former residence, presumably demonstrating Musharaf's loyalty to the slain leader and to the close ties to India he represented. This was the interpretation of JSD, which, although leftist, opposed close ties with either New Delhi or Moscow. On the evening of November 4, the news leaked out in Dhaka that the four senior BAKSAL leaders held in Dhaka Central Jail (Tajuddin Ahmad, Syed Nazrul Islam, A.H.M. Kamruzzaman, and Mansur Ali) had been killed. The question of who killed them and why has not been satisfactorily answered.

The JSD aroused the soldiers in Dhaka cantonment and instigated a revolt against Musharaf on the night of November 6. Musharaf was killed in a firefight on November 7. Although the sepoys looked toward Zia for leadership, it appears that he was not directly involved. Zia was reinstated as chief of staff. Mushtaque refused to resume the presidency, asking the nation to follow Sayem, who, although a civilian, became chief martial law administrator (CMLA) as well as president. Zia and the chiefs of the naval and air staffs were made deputy CMLAs. For the time being, the four men divided the cabinet portfolios among themselves.

Zia rewarded JSD support for the second coup of November by releasing several party leaders who had been jailed by Mujib. The JSD was not content with this, however, and attempted to implement the radical "people's army" system they advocated. The demands listed in their twelve-point program included the formation of revolutionary committees in each unit that would pyramid into a national committee to decide military policy. Zia resisted this demand, and later in the month he rearrested a number of JSD leaders. He also arrested Colonel Abu Taher, a freedom fighter and head of the military front of the JSD. Taher was eventually tried for inciting rebellion among the soldiers and executed in July 1976. The majors who killed Mujib settled in Libya.

THE ZIA REGIME

Zia quickly emerged as the leader of the new government. Although Sayem was not totally inactive as president, his age and health limited his activities. Sayem did announce upon his assumption of office that his government would follow the election program spelled out by Mushtaque, but elections were delayed by Zia from 1977 to 1978 for the presidential election and to 1979 for the parliamentary election.

Zia's transformation from a military leader who could control the country, if necessary, with the coercive means at his command to a charismatic popular political figure surprised most observers. His name was well known from his role in the liberation war, but he had seemed to accept without question the degrading of his personal position by Mujib and had to be persuaded to accept the leadership after the second November coup and resume his post as army chief of staff. Zia was the principal of the three military deputy CMLAs, as he led the major portion of the military establishment. He took responsibility for the ministries of finance and home affairs. The former is hardly a base for projecting a political personality—although it is concerned with all ministries, but the home portfolio gave Zia direct supervision over the police and intelligence services and put him in control of political activities. Zia acted more and more as a political figure, traveling extensively, exhorting the people to higher levels of production, and spreading the politics of hope in a nation that seemed to have little to hope for. He probably saw more of Bangladesh in his travels than any previous leader, including Fazlul Huq and Mujib.

The law-and-order situation improved greatly under Zia. Zia ended the favoritism that Mujib had displayed toward Awami Leaguers, and law enforcement by both military and civil courts gave a greater sense of security, although civil rights were curtailed under the martial law system. The Zia regime arrested relatively fewer persons than the Mujib regime in its last days. The prison population began gradually to decline. A continuing problem with some armed groups—especially that led by Kader "Tiger" Siddiqi, one-time freedom fighter and former enlisted man in the Pakistan Army, was eased when the Janata Party came to power in India in early 1977. Morarji Desai and his associates discontinued the assistance and sanctuary that Indira Gandhi's government had given to the pro-Mujib rebels.

Reorganizing the Government and the Military

The Zia regime utilized all of the civil service and specialized cadres available to Bangladesh. Mujib, as described, refused to take full advantage of those who had remained at their posts during the war or who were caught in West Pakistan in 1971. The few arrested after the August and November coups were soon restored to duty. It is, of course, not unusual that with civilian politicians out of the way, the civil service should join hands with the military to provide "expert" government. Shafiul Azam, the most senior of those recalled, was named to head the Planning Commission. He later served as a minister under both Zia and Ershad. The addition of these restored officers to those who had worked with Mujib, coupled with the removal of Mujib's political appointees to the civil service, greatly toned up the higher ranks of administration—the secretariat officers and the higher divisional and district officials. The middle and lower echelons of the Bangladeshi civil service remained severely under-trained, often guilty of petty corruption, and badly underpaid. Proposed training schemes—the most recent (1983) to be funded through a World Bank loan—are being implemented, but so far with little effect.

Zia also moved to integrate the armed forces, giving returnees a status appropriate to their qualifications and seniority. This angered some of the freedom fighters who had reached high positions more rapidly than they would otherwise have expected to. The usual solution in dealing with the problem officers was to send them on diplomatic assignments. Zia made repatriate Major General Husain Muhammad Ershad the deputy chief of staff. He had difficulty with the air force chief slot. Air Vice-Marshal M. G. Tawab attempted in April 1976 to use the majors who had killed Mujib to mount a coup against Zia. Zia got wind of the threat and acted first. He dismissed and exiled Tawab replacing him with Air Vice-Marshal M. K. Bashar. Bashar was killed in an aircraft crash in September 1976. The next incumbent was Air Vice-Marshal A. G. Mahmud, who was also displaced in October 1977.

The initial cabinet included only Sayem and the three military chiefs. By January 1976, however, most of the portfolios were in the hands of civilians, who were termed "advisers" rather than "ministers." Some positions were retained by the president or the marital law deputies. President Sayem held the defense and foreign affairs portfolios until the presidency passed to Zia in April 1977. Zia retained the home portfolio until July 1978, and was defense minister until his death. The food ministry went with the air chief position until July 1977. The naval chief, Admiral M. H. Khan, was also minister of power, flood control, and water resources until November 1977.

Many of the new ministers had experience either in government, in their fields, or in both, and much of that experience had been gained during the days of united Pakistan. The constitution, which continued in force except as modified by martial law or as amended by decree, provided that the president could name a vice-president. Sayem did not, but in June 1977 Zia appointed as his vice-president Justice Abdus Sattar, a political figure active before and after independence. Sattar had briefly been a member of the Second Constituent Assembly and a minister in 1956. He was appointed to the High Court of East Pakistan in 1957, and to the Supreme Court in 1968. As chief election commissioner in 1969, Sattar ran the 1970 election. He became a special assistant to Sayem in 1975, and adviser for law and parliamentary affairs in February 1977, a post he held throughout the Zia period in addition to the vice-presidency. One of the first civilians to join the cabinet was Mirza Nurul Huda, who became minister of commerce in December 1975. Huda had been a professor of economics, then minister of finance and very briefly governor of East Pakistan. He replaced Zia in finance in December 1978. One of Bangladesh's outstanding educators, Muhammad Shamsul Huq, who had been a minister under Yahya, took Sayem's post as foreign minister when Zia replaced Sayem as president in April 1977. Additional members were added as time passed, and as preparations for elections began, many were drawn from political groups.

Political Activity Resumes

Mushtaque and Sayem had both pledged that political activity would begin in August 1976, in anticipation of elections the following February. Mushtaque had left the Awami League and formed the Democratic League. Some of the leftist parties—whose electoral showing had been dismal in the past—opposed the resumption of political activity. Some of the military, not surprisingly, thought the date was much too soon. Sayem held firm, however, and political activity, severely circumscribed, did begin on schedule. Almost sixty parties applied for recognition, and initially twenty-one were approved, a number that swelled greatly as time went on. In November 1976, it was announced by the government that elections would be postponed. This was done over Sayem's objection, and he resigned the position of CMLA to Zia. Many parties and political leaders also objected, including the Democratic League and Mushtaque, and several of Mushtaque's associates were arrested.

Having consolidated his position in the army, Zia became president on April 21, 1977, when Sayem resigned on the grounds of ill health. Zia now held the dominant position in the country. He was supported by the vast majority of Bangladeshis and opposed only by some political figures who saw a greater chance for influence in a revived parliamentary system. In his first address as president, Zia renewed the pledge to hold elections but did not set a specific date.

With his base seemingly secure, Zia drew on his popularity to espouse a clearly political program. In April 1977, he announced a nineteen-point program, following the Bangladeshi penchant for specifically numbered manifestos. The key to Zia's policy was increasing Bangladeshi production, especially in food grains, and integrating rural development through a variety of programs, of which population planning was the most important. In a whirlwind campaign, Zia presented this manifesto to the people, and on May 30 faced the electorate in a referendum on his continuance in office. The results showed that 88.5 percent of the electorate turned out, with 98.9 percent voting for Zia. The referendum, however, was viewed by Bangladeshis as a stunt rather than as a genuine expression of opinion. The obvious question was "What if Zia had lost?"

Nonpartisan elections had been held for local government officials in January 1977. The referendum seemed to belie reports that many of those elected had sympathies with the Awami League. In any event, Zia used the newly elected councillors as a means to develop a following and, to a lesser degree, a rural political organization.

It was clear that Zia had political ambitions that much of the nation supported. He would need to form a political party to back his presidency and supply him with a working majority in a new parliament. Zia looked to the past, working for a time with former chief minister Ataur Rahman Khan, who had left the Awami League before the 1970 elections in a dispute for leadership with Mujib, and who would therefore not carry a Mujibist outlook into the Zia camp. Another possible ally was Mushtaque, but he and Zia did not get along, and there was a danger of the question of the unpunished majors surfacing. (As it turned out, in 1977 Mushtaque was charged with corruption in office, convicted, and jailed.) Zia encouraged Vice-President Sattar to take the lead in forming a new political party, but before Sattar could act, the tranquillity of the country and the security of Zia were challenged.

The Dhaka Mutiny

In late September 1977, the Japanese Red Army hijacked a Japan Air Lines aircraft and forced it to land in Dhaka. On September 30, while the attention of the government was riveted on this event, a mutiny broke out in Bogra. (The coincidence was most likely accidental. Reports of possible collusion between the Red Army and the mutineers seem implausible.) The minor mutiny was quelled quickly, although three officers were killed. Reports of the event were generally ignored in Dhaka; there had been several such incidents since the coups of November 1975. On the night of October 2, however, a major mutiny occurred in Dhaka. The mutineers attacked Zia's residence (which was successfully defended by his guards), captured Dhaka Radio for a short time, and killed a number of air force officers at Dhaka airport, where many were gathered for the negotiations connected with the hijacking. Air Vice-Marshal Mahmud was spared. The army quickly organized itself and put down the rebellion, but the government was severely shaken. Mahmud was removed from the food ministry and from his air force post. The mutineers were primarily air force enlisted men.

The shock to the government was that intelligence sources did not discover the likelihood of a plot, even in the wake of the Bogra incident. The military and the civil intelligence chiefs were both removed. Three of the aspirants to the army chief of staff post held by Zia were transferred or retired; one of them would lead the successful plot against Zia in 1981. Who instigated the coup is still not clearly known, although some evidence indicates that the JSD was involved, and possibly soldiers loyal to the majors who had rebelled against Mujib. The government quickly recovered its aplomb, but the public and international nature of the Dhaka incident would haunt Zia and his associates.

Presidential and Parliamentary Elections

After the Dhaka mutiny, political normalization resumed. Zia would now be described as "president" and not "major general," and his military colleagues in the cabinet were to resign either their military or their cabinet positions; they could not retain both. Thirteen new appointees to the cabinet from the political ranks were given lesser ministries. They worked with Sattar to form a party. Zia announced that he would run in the forthcoming elections, supported by a "national front." The main ingredient of the front would be the Jatiyo Ganatantrik Dal (JAGODAL, the National Democratic Party), founded in February 1978. Besides the new ministers, most of the founders were either political unknowns or persons who had long been disassociated from political activity. The party favored a presidential form of government, in accord with the final form under Mujib but without the restrictive rules he had framed.

In April 1978, an ordinance set the rules for a presidential election on June 3. Zia would be the candidate of the JAGODAL-led Nationalist Front. This alliance was a strange mixture of leftist (including the pro-Beijing National Awami Party) and rightist (including the now-legal Bangladesh Muslim League) groups. Opposed to this front was a front that supported General M.A.G. Osmany, the leader of the Mukti Bahini during the liberation war. Osmany had resigned from the Awami League in opposition to the formation of BAKSAL by Mujib, but the Awami League was now a member of his front. Osmany supported a return to parliamentary government but chided the Awami League, his partner, for BAKSAL and for the excesses of the Mujib regime. Odder combinations can scarcely be imagined. Zia trounced Osmany with 76.7 percent of the vote to the latter's 21.7 percent, with the balance going to several little-known candidates. Zia's position was henceforth legitimately based on a contested election, which seems to have been fairly conducted.

The council of advisers was transformed into a council of ministers that included representatives of the parties supporting Zia plus sixteen holdovers from the earlier group. Masihur Rahman, leader of the National Awami Party, was designated "senior minister" and given a status just below President Zia and Vice-President Sattar. The Awami League divided shortly after the election, with the smaller faction disavowing the more extreme positions taken by Mujib. Zia also changed JAGODAL into a new party that included major portions of the other parties in the Nationalist Front. The new party, which was named the Bangladesh Nationalist Party (BNP), was headed by Sattar.

Parliamentary elections were held in February 1979. After major campaigning by Zia, the BNP won 207 of the 300 seats in parliament with about 44 percent of the vote. The larger faction of the Awami League won 39 seats with 25 percent of the vote, making it the official opposition. The Muslim League members who had not combined with the BNP joined a coalition with the Islamic Democratic League, taking 20 seats with 8 percent of the vote. The remaining seats were scattered among a number of smaller parties, some of them rumps of the parties that had joined the BNP. Shah Azizur

Rahman became prime minister in place of Masihur Rahman, who died suddenly just as the election was ending.

Zia's Legacy

Zia continued to inspire Bangladesh as the country made considerable progress in economic development and also made its mark in international and regional affairs. His failure, which became clear after his assassination, was in not building an effective party organization. Zia shared an affliction common among leaders who have gained power in unsettled political systems. He failed to select and groom a credible first lieutenant to succeed him eventually. Sattar, seventy-five and ailing at Zia's death, was not a credible successor. Zia had appointed a prime minister, Shah Azizur Rahman, but Aziz's frequent party shifts in the past may have made him politically suspect. Zia could also have chosen Badruddoza Chaudhury, who was first named senior deputy prime minister and then secretary general of the BNP. Another possibility was Moudud Ahmad, a deputy prime minister who eventually was dismissed in December 1979.

It is not our purpose here to suggest any single person as a credible successor, but to point out that Zia's failure left a void in the party as well as the government when he was murdered. Attention to party organization at the lower administrative and constituency levels was also largely ignored, to the extent that with the possibility of a new election in 1984 the BNP is divided and unprepared to face a new test. Parliamentarians and others rode on Zia's coattails, following the pattern in eastern Bengal, East Pakistan, and Bangladesh of large victories by a party with a single leader, a single issue, or both. This pattern has been evident in each election beginning with that of 1937.

Zia was assassinated in Chittagong on May 30, 1981, in a plot allegedly masterminded by Major General Muhammad Manzur, the army commander in Chittagong. Manzur had earlier been chief of the general staff, and had been transferred to Chittagong in the aftermath of the October 1977 mutiny. He was scheduled for a new transfer to a noncommand position in Dhaka, and apparently his disappointment over this, coupled with his visions of grandeur and personal hostility toward Zia, was the motivation for his action. The army, under Chief of Staff Major General Ershad, remained loyal to the Dhaka government and put down the rebellion, killing Manzur, his wife, and many others. In the trials that followed, a sizable number of officers and enlisted men received the death penalty for complicity.

THE SATTAR INTERLUDE

In the immediate aftermath of the assassination, the government of Bangladesh acted as the constitution provided that it should. Vice-President Abdus Sattar became acting president. He declared that an election would be held within 180 days, as required, to select a successor for a new five-year term. Sattar retained the Zia cabinet, although he dropped a few members before the election. Ershad remained army chief of staff and was praised for containing the rebellion quickly and effectively.

The factionalism of the BNP was brought into the open by the process of selecting a presidential candidate. Many felt that because of Sattar's age handicap, he should be eliminated from consideration. Other contenders included Prime Minister Shah Azizur Rahman, BNP Secretary General (and former deputy prime minister) Badruddoza Chaudhury, and Moudud Ahmad, also a former deputy prime minister. Ahmad had been dropped by Zia in a disagreement over party discipline but retained a strong group of followers. The dispute over the candidacy led to the dismissal of some members from the cabinet, including Moudud Ahmad, who saw himself as a potential candidate— a view not shared by others. Unable to agree on a younger nominee, the BNP selected Sattar, although many thought they would soon have to repeat the process.

Sattar faced thirty-eight other candidates, most of them political nonentities. General Osmany ran again but without the support of the Awami League, which as noted above had divided soon after the presidential election. The larger faction was headed by Hasina Wajid, a daughter of Mujib's who had returned from exile in India to lead the party. Rather than choose her as the candidate, the Awami League selected Kamal Husain, a minister of law and parliamentary affairs and later of foreign affairs under Mujib. Husain had spent much of the time since Mujib's death out of the country. The result of the election in November gave Sattar 65.5 percent of the votes counted and Kamal Husain 26.0 percent, with the other 8.5 percent scattered among the other thirty-seven candidates.

Sattar thus became the duly elected president of the country. He chose Mirza Nurul Huda, who had left Zia's cabinet in April 1980, as vice-president, and made several changes in the cabinet. Shah Azizur Rahman, who continued as prime minister, reportedly sought to establish himself as Sattar's logical replacement and thereby secure the candidacy in the next round of voting.

The new president was clearly from the civilian side of government. The link that Zia, even after dropping the chief of staff post, had maintained with the military was broken. Immediately after the election, Ershad, now Lieutenant General Ershad, demanded an institutionalized role in governing the country. Sattar initially responded in a press conference that he saw no role for the military other than defending the country, but in January 1981, faced with the prospect of a coup led by Ershad, Sattar agreed to set up a national security council with the president, vice-president, and prime minister representing the civilian side and the three service chiefs representing the military. The council would be the ultimate authority if the internal or external security of the country was endangered, but it was clear that Ershad envisioned a broader decision-making capability. At the presumed behest of Ershad and the military, Sattar realigned his cabinet in February, dropping several ministers—some for alleged corruption.

Apparently, Ershad was being pressured by his colleagues to exercise greater power. The military had considered Zia one of their own—or, at least, most had—but Sattar was a civilian. Rumors of a coup were widespread. On March 24, 1982, Ershad assumed full powers under martial law; suspended (but did not abrogate) the constitution; dismissed Sattar and Vice-President Mohammadullah, who had just replaced Huda; dissolved the cabinet and the parliament; and became chief martial law administrator with the naval and air chiefs as his deputies. On March 27, an almost unknown justice, Abul Fazal Muhammad Ahsanuddin Chaudhury, was sworn in as president. Ershad also assumed the title "president of the council of ministers," that is, prime minister.

ERSHAD'S MARTIAL LAW

When Mushtaque and Zia took power, there was general relief and a widespread belief that things under Mujib had been so bad and the November 1975 coups so violent that there was a justification for change. No such feeling accompanied the takeover by Ershad. He was seen by many as a power-hungry general who lacked the skills that Zia had developed, having been kept in Zia's shadow. Sattar, unlike Mushtaque and Zia, had been legitimately elected president; Ershad was a usurper who had overruled the people's democratic expression.

Ershad justified his action, which most but not all of the military supported, in terms reminiscent of many a military coup. He said the security of the country was threatened by social and political indiscipline, unprecedented corruption, a devastated economy, an administrative stalemate, extreme deterioration of law and order, and frightening economic and food crises. "At this critical juncture of the country, the patriotic Armed Forces had to respond to the call of the people by taking this extreme measure, for the nation has no other alternative."[2] He said his government would tackle the economic and food problems and would improve internal security. He also promised that when proper conditions were restored elections would be held and power returned to the people.

Ershad appointed a council of advisers (later ministers) to work with him. Some were quite distinguished and had served the country before. Several were retired or retiring civil servants, including A.M.A. Muhith and A.Z.M. Obaidullah Khan. Two of those dismissed after the October 1977 mutiny—Air Vice-Marshal Mahmud and former head of military intelligence Air Vice-Marshal Aminul Islam—were restored. At the same time, Ershad had a number of Sattar's ministers arrested on charges of corruption. Many of the arrests seemed vindictive, and the charges were probably false. Some of the ministers have been convicted by military tribunals, others acquitted. Political figures such as former deputy prime minister Moudud Ahmad have been harassed. The trend under Zia toward a sharp reduction of political prisoners has been reversed under Ershad.

There has been some minimal economic progress since Ershad took office and some international achievements, which have generally built upon Zia's accomplishments. Ershad's program of denigrating Zia has been widely disapproved in Bangladesh. He has dismantled some of the positive institutions introduced by Zia, including the gram sarkars (village governments) that Zia had designated to assist in development planning and implementation. The key adviser to Zia on the village government program was dismissed. Ershad reorganized the ministries, perhaps for the sake of efficiency, but it may just have been change for change's sake.

The festering internal security problem in the Chittagong Hill Tracts District has plagued Ershad as it had his predecessors. The district covers about one-eleventh of the area of Bangladesh; has the only developed source of hydroelectric power, on the Karnaphuli River; and is potentially a major source of timber. The small population, about 750,000 in 1981, is largely tribal and Buddhist, with some Hindu groups as well. The largest of the tribes, which inhabits the north of the district, is the Chakma. (The raja of the Chakma won one of the two seats lost by the Awami League in 1970; he has since lived in Pakistan, but his mother was a member of Zia's cabinet for a time.)

The ongoing conflict is not untypical of tribal-settled relations. Population pressure in the lowlands and economic opportunities in the hill areas have led Bengalis to move into the tribal area, to the detriment of the tribes. Most of the small trading is in the hands of lowlanders, as is much of the existing timber trade. Much land was submerged when the dam was completed in 1961. The tribes demand that their land be left alone and that migration be stopped. In the British period, the area was declared off limits to lowlanders but enforcement was and still is lax. The tribal area is also adjacent to disturbed areas in India, and there may have been some foreign involvement from India and in India from Pakistan before Bangladeshi independence. Armed insurrection has also been encouraged by leftists in Bangladesh, including one group led by a former freedom fighter who was associated with Colonel Abu Taher and the JSD. The rebels' goal has been autonomy for the Hill Tracts, although some demand independence.

The government has responded to sporadic rebellion in the area both with military means and with educational, social, and economic proposals. The army has been unable to pacify the area completely despite considerable effort. The nonmilitary proposals often entail the development of area timber resources, which, unless they are managed very carefully, can quickly become depleted. Education often involves removing students from their native environment and putting them in cities where they have difficulty adapting. Social change can only weaken the strong cultural ties that have held the tribes together, and it is therefore resisted. The problem has been a drain on the economy of Bangladesh for which no easy solution exists.

Ershad, like earlier martial law rulers, has been unable to stifle the Bengali desire for political activity. Bengal was often described as the most politicized province of India, and although political activity diminished somewhat after 1970, it is still strong. Political parties are officially banned, but political confabulations continue apace. Factionalism in the BNP and the Awami League has worsened, and the Muslim League split in 1977. Despite this factionalism, negotiations for possible future cooperation between parties continue at almost every social gathering of the Dhaka elite.

In November 1983, just before a visit by Queen Elizabeth II and just after his own visit to the United States, Ershad announced that presidential elections would be held on May 24, 1984, to be followed by parliamentary elections on November 25. The opposition parties have demanded that parliamentary elections precede the presidential election, for the obvious reason that they expect Ershad to win the presidency and then use his influence to ensure majority support of him in the parliament. Ershad has yielded partially to the demand by scheduling both presidential and parliamentary elections on May 27, 1984. This will presumably mean the end of martial law if nothing goes awry.

Ershad has indicated that he wishes to enter politics as Zia did, and he will need a political party to support him. It is likely that we will see a rerun of the JAGODAL and BNP developments with different names and somewhat different casts. Ershad made a turn toward Islamic political philosophy early in his rule but seems to have reversed this, and he may attempt to mobilize much the same type of following as Zia did. Many in the BNP were there for opportunistic reasons and probably will find little problem in switching. How strong their following will be without the charismatic Zia to lead them is a question the election returns will answer. Ershad has little of Zia's charismatic appeal. He is unlikely to turn to the Awami League for support unless he is willing to adopt that party's pro-Indian and, to a degree, pro-Soviet views, its long-standing demand that the majors responsible for Mujib's death be punished, and its socialist and secular stance on domestic matters. This would presumably be hard for Ershad to do.

At this writing, the future political development is hard to predict. Ershad's bland personality is one problem. Another is his generally lackluster performance in comparison with Zia. And finally, Ershad appears to preach the "politics of despair," as opposed to the "politics of hope" that Zia represented, expounding hard work and self-reliance as the means to the development of Bangladesh.

NOTES

1. The phrase "international basket case" was widely used in Washington just after independence. It has been attributed, perhaps incorrectly, to Henry Kissinger.

2. Ershad's speech was reported in *Bangladesh Today*, published by the High Commission of Bangladesh, London, March 15–31, 1982.

6

Administration: Civil and Military

A major task for a new nation-state is what some political scientists call "state building"—the establishment of an administrative system to perform the duties essential to the operation of the government, within the boundaries controlled and recognized by the international system. Bangladesh had to set up a civil administration in the war-torn nation very quickly.

CIVIL ADMINISTRATIVE MACHINERY

The centralized administrative system of Bangladesh is based on the Mughal, British, and Pakistani patterns of the past. The provinces have shared power at times, when the writ of Mughal Delhi was weak and when the British deliberately attempted to devolve power at the provincial level—for example, after the Government of India Acts of 1919 and 1935. Bengal may have chafed under this system, but there have been only two major armed rebellions against the central power: in 1740, during the period of the later Mughals, and in 1971.

Recruitment to the higher levels of government service has also been centralized, and civil service positions are coveted for the power and prestige that go with membership in an elite service. The Mughals often rewarded their civil servants with land grants; the British granted knighthoods and similar honors; Pakistan favored its top administrators with special considerations such as land, loans for homes, and even decorations. Government service became almost a dynastic matter as sons followed fathers into the service, sometimes at a higher level, and intermarrriage among members of this new caste became a means to perpetuate the lineage. In the 1960s, a British diplomat compiled family trees—much in the tradition of earlier British publications for both Great Britain and India—that trace the interlocking of one hundred prominent Pakistani families from Ayub down. Intermarriage assured the continuation of professions of prestige and power. The documents show a large number of linkages between families of East and West Pakistan and between East Pakistani and West Bengali Muslims, although this was more common among the Urdu-speaking elite than among the vernacular families.

The pattern remains evident in Bangladesh today. It almost seems as if all leading civil servants are related to one another, and to the industrial, educational, and professional elites. This elitism is often credited more to West than to East Pakistan, but the evidence shows otherwise. The elite tends to use English as a public means of communication, despite the efforts at Bengalization that began under Mujib and were not entirely curtailed under Zia. The cultural and educational gap between the rulers and the ruled has changed little since the time when Persian or Urdu was the elite language. This division may also be seen in the allocations for university-level education as opposed to rural primary education, noted below.

Elitism has not made the administration insensitive to the needs of the country; often quite the contrary has been true. In contrast to Pakistan, where many administrators are drawn from urban-based elites, almost all Bangladeshi civil servants retain close ties to the rural area of their ancestry. Usually their families left the village only one or two generations ago. Nonetheless, university-learned and foreign-derived solutions to rural problems are difficult to communicate to the rural citizenry or even to locally based lower-level civil servants. Part of the communication problem is mechanical: There are not enough working telephones or radios.

Bangladeshis use the quaint phrase "erstwhile CSP" to describe former members of the highest level of the central services before independence, a level on a par with the Pakistan Foreign Service and a notch above the Police Service of Pakistan. A large number of other central services were based on specialized cadres, such as the income tax and customs services, and on technical specialists, such as agricultural, forest, educational, and health groups. Within the CSP there was also an economic pool, which staffed the Planning Commission, the ministries of finance and commerce, and similar bodies at the central and provincial levels. As officers recruited before 1947 retired and recruitment became more balanced, the proportion of East Pakistanis in the CSP had gradually increased to almost 40 percent by the time of Bangladeshi independence. As almost all had been recruited after 1947, they had not reached the highest ranks in numbers anywhere equal to the refugees or West Pakistanis. As noted earlier, Mujib failed to use this pool of talent effectively. Zia reversed Mujib's policy, but a shortage remained, especially after he dismissed politically appointed officers. At the highest rank of secretary, Zia appointed a substantial number of police officers to supplement the available "erstwhile CSP" officers.

Below the central civil service cadres were the provincial civil service cadres, examined and appointed from Calcutta before 1947 and from Dhaka after that. The police also had a provincial cadre, as did many of the other specialized and technical services whose work was of both a central and a provincial nature. Provincial officers were recruited at a lower level—although a college degree was required—and filled less prestigious posts than those held by the central service officers. The deputy commissioner of a district was generally a junior central service officer or a very senior, specially selected provincial officer. The same was true for district police superintendents.

At the lower echelons are government employees recruited by the province and generally assigned to their local areas to oversee various financial, revenue, and police functions. At the bottom are the clerical and support personnel. A college education is rarely required for these two lowest levels. These employees, who have the most contact with people who need government services, often do not receive proper on-the-job training to perform these services. They are usually underpaid and frequently supplement their income through corruption. Efficiency in government is not a strong point in Bangladesh; overemployment and underutilization are endemic. Training may improve the situation, but there is also a need, much more difficult to achieve, for higher morale. The serious corruption problem includes not only bribery but nonmonetary incentives as well.

As president, Zia provided Bangladesh with a single unified civil service system not unlike that of the United States. All positions are scheduled at a specific grade on the scale. Recruitment is possible at several entry levels, though an examination is necessary at the higher entry points. The entry points correspond to the former levels of the CSP and other central services, the former provincial service, and the lower echelons. Promotion is possible all along the line, although it is extraordinarily unlikely that someone entering at the bottom could reach the top.

Zia also introduced a combined training system, which is still being implemented. This is a particularly important need for the Bangladeshi civil service and will take time and funds to implement fully. During the British period, the emphasis for district officers was on revenue collection and law and order (hence the titles district collector and district magistrate have coexisted with deputy commissioner). In Bangladesh, the need is for greater emphasis on general administration and coordination for development. These skills were not developed in training for the earlier service. Government responsibility to the people is something that will take time to ingrain in the habits of state employees.

The standard unit of administration has been the district, but the Ershad regime is in the process of upgrading the thana to the standard unit of government. In Bengal's long-standing administrative system, the thana stood above the village and below the subdivision, the district, and the division. The term is originally a police designation for a local station.

Bangladesh is organized into four divisions and twenty districts: Chittagong Division, comprising Chittagong, Chittagong Hill Tracts, Noakhali, Comilla (named Tippera in the British period), and Sylhet districts; Dhaka, comprising Dhaka, Faridpur, Mymensingh, Jamalpur, and Tangail; Khulna, comprising Khulna, Jessore, Kushtia, Barisal, and Patuakhali; and Rajshahi, comprising Rajshahi, Dinajpur, Pabna, Rangpur, and Bogra. Most of the districts were inherited from the British; exceptions are Kushtia, which is the portion of the former Nadia District awarded to Pakistan, and Sylhet, which includes most of the former Sylhet District of Assam Province. After independence in 1947 two former subdivisions of Mymensingh District, Tangail and Jamalpur, were made independent districts, and the former Bakerganj District was divided into Barisal and Patuakhali districts. Below the district are subdivisions and then thanas. The Mushtaque government canceled Mujib's plan, formed just at the end of his rule, to create fifty districts, each with its own governor.

At the national level the Bangladeshi government is organized into the usual ministries and departments. Each department is headed by a secretary or, in the case of smaller units, by a slightly less senior official, an additional secretary. One or more departments will form a ministry, with a single political head. Below the rank of additional secretary are joint secretaries, deputy secretaries, and section officers. Independent units concerned with specific tasks—for example, the publicly owned corporations—are common in the economic area.

THE MILITARY AND THE POLICE

The rift between those who fought for independence in 1971 and those trapped in West Pakistan at the time has plagued the military since independence. Another source of division was Mujib's creation of his own personal force, the Jatiyo Rakhi Bahini, which received preferential treatment in supply and pay. The Rakhi Bahini no longer exists, but the division between freedom fighters and "returnees" remains, although the number of senior freedom fighters has declined through retirement and diversion to other posts, often overseas as heads of diplomatic missions. Ershad himself is a "returnee," as are many of his close associates. The differences between the two groups will not be fully bridged until a postindependence generation of officers reaches the highest ranks—a distant prospect.

The radicalism that has surfaced at times among enlisted men also continues to cast a shadow. The influence of the JSD in the military is difficult to estimate, but the party had some role in putting Zia into power, and was probably also involved in the September and October 1977 mutinies at Bogra and Dhaka. The formation of a "people's army" is unlikely to occur except through a violent revolution, but it remains a goal for the JSD sympathizers.

The army has about 75,000 officers and enlisted men. They are organized primarily into divisions, with headquarters at Dhaka, Chittagong, Comilla, Jessore, and Bogra. A military academy has been established at Comilla. Recruitment of both officers and enlisted men has been expanded greatly since the Pakistan period, when the military was not considered an important career avenue for young men. The army is poorly equipped, although a munitions factory north of Dhaka does produce some equipment. Arms imports are severely restricted by the limited availability of foreign exchange.

The navy has added a single British-built frigate to its fleet of patrol boats. Although naval headquarters is in Dhaka, the principal base for naval operations is, of course, in Chittagong. There are between 4,000 and 5,000 sailors in the navy.

The air force is also poorly equipped. Its headquarters is in Dhaka, but Bangladesh has several other usable airfields. In 1983, fighting aircraft included 8 MiG-21s (2 of which are trainers) supplied by the Soviet Union during the Mujib period. These are believed to be in almost inoperable condition, partly as a result of a cutoff of spare parts. In 1977–1978, China supplied 30 F-6s (the Chinese version of the Soviet MiG-19), most of which are still operable. In addition, the air force has several French-built jet trainers and 4 Soviet-supplied transport aircraft (1 AN-24 and 3 AN-26s), which also date from the Mujib period. Helicopters include 6 U.S. Bell 212s (twin-engine Hueys), 4 MiG-8s from the Soviet Union, and 4 Indian-made, French-designed Chetaks. The helicopters serve a number of purposes in the civilian sector, in addition to their military use in the Chittagong Hill Tracts. The personnel of the air force numbers about 2,500.

Bangladesh has two paramilitary forces. One, the Bangladesh Rifles (successors to the East Pakistan Rifles), is formally charged with border patrol duties and numbers about 25,000 to 30,000 lightly armed men. Armed even more lightly and inferior in organization and training are the Ansars, a sort of national guard based in the villages. There may be as many as 15,000 men in the Ansars.

For internal security, the government relies primarily on the Bangladesh Police. Except for the Ansars, the police are generally considered the lowest in the pecking order of security forces, and although their officers rank high in the civil service system and are well trained, the lower ranks are often poorly trained, poorly equipped, and poorly paid. The police have much more contact with the citizens than the army, and therefore take the brunt of criticism when they are called upon to quell disturbances. The East Pakistan Police had been assisted by the United States until scandals in Vietnam forced the termination of the public safety program. Improved training, better equipment, and greater responsibility toward the public are clearly needed. There are about 35,000 men in the Bangladesh Police.

7

Economic and
Social Development

This chapter will survey the Bangladeshi economy and society as they have changed since independence and as they exist in 1984. Bangladesh is properly called the "largest, poorest" nation in the world, but conditions have been evolving, however slightly, in the little more than a decade since the ties with Pakistan were broken. The social environment has changed but little, and it is in this context that both political and economic development must be seen.

THE ECONOMY

The two most important economic and socioeconomic goals for Bangladesh are achieving self-sufficiency in food grains, especially rice, and slowing the rate of population growth. The two are intimately related. The amount of cultivable land is basically constant, affected only by increasing the quantity by double or triple cropping; hence, as the population increases the land per person decreases. The challenge is to increase production per unit of land at a faster rate than the population growth rate.[1]

The land system provides that no family may own more than 33 acres of land. This means little to the overwhelming majority of Bangladeshis: According to the 1977 agricultural census, only 0.4 percent of farmers owned more than 25 acres, accounting for 3.4 percent of the total cultivated land. The average farm holding was 3.5 acres, but when the landless are factored into the calculation, the average holding is only 2.3 acres. The landless, if they have no other occupation, are dependent for income, in kind and in cash, upon farm labor opportunities. Of those who hold land, 58.3 percent own the land they till; a little more than 0.5 percent only rent land. The remainder farm a combination of owned and rented land. The rented land has much greater permanence than it had in the days of Cornwallis, as acts passed over the years have permitted most rented land to pass from generation to generation. The inheritance patterns of both Hindus and Muslims have led to great fragmentation of holdings so that the average 3.5 acres are not in a single consolidated piece. Most holdings contain 6 to 9 fragments, and about 10 percent contain 20 or more.

A growing proportion of arable land is now tilled two or three times a year, thus expanding the effective cultivated acreage. Nevertheless, about 55 percent of the land is still single-cropped; 38 percent is double-cropped and 7 percent is triple-cropped. Cropping more than once depends both on the possibility of growing a variety of crops and on the availability of irrigation water outside the monsoon rainy season. Throughout the country the cropping intensity is about 1.5, but there are wide variations from region to region. In 1977 about 30 percent of the holdings reported using irrigation water, accounting for about 31 percent of the cropped area. Except for the very smallest holdings—those less than 0.5 acre—there was not significant variance in irrigation use between larger and smaller holdings. Land is irrigated by surface water, most often by inundation canals and occasionally by much more expensive lift pump systems using human, animal, diesel, or electric power; or from wells, some of them modern tubewells using electric or diesel pumps.

There are proposals for additional land reforms both to increase the land of many who have clearly uneconomic holdings and to distribute land to the landless. The smallest landholders and the landless are seen as a potential dissident group that could be mobilized against the government and its supporters, who are assumed to include the larger landholders and the urban elites to whom they are often related. A 1978 study by the government of Bangladesh (varying slightly from the 1977 agricultural census) states that 14.7 percent of rural households are landless, except for "homestead" land, and that another 44.7 percent own less than one acre, a total of 59.4 percent at this clearly below-subsistence level. The census defines a small holding as 2.5 acres or less and states that 49.7 percent are in that category, but this excludes the landless. Another 40.9 percent of landholders are in the medium category, with 2.5 to 7.5 acres; the remaining 9.4 percent hold more than 7.5 acres. Clearly, there is not much land available to redistribute. In 1977, two-fifths of landholders already were in what might, under the local circumstances, be con-

PHOTO 7.1 A village scene in Jessore District. The fields contain winter (boro) rice; in the background the palm tree is being tapped for its sap. The man in the foreground carries a wooden plow. (Courtesy of Rudolph von Bernuth)

sidered a socially desirable range. With continuing inheritance the larger holdings (over 7.5 acres) will become smaller.

The political problem cannot be ignored, although the organization and radicalization of the lowest strata of rural Bangladesh seems unlikely for the present, especially on a nationwide basis. To many observers, the answers appear to lie in economic solutions such as increasing output, consolidating divided holdings, and expanding employment opportunities in nonfarm areas and in agroindustry. These solutions, of course, may prove as difficult to realize as increasing the holdings of small landholders and the landless.

"Miracle rice" did not expand production in East Pakistan to nearly the extent "miracle wheat" did in the Punjab. The smaller holdings and correspondingly lower amounts of funds available to capitalize on the new technology contrasted sharply with the situation in the Punjab. It is often said that the farmers of the eastern subcontinent are more resistant to change than those in the northwest, and there may be something to this. The Ayub government did expend considerable energy on agricultural development in the east, but the starting base was also much lower in the east. The destruction of the civil war left independent Bangladesh with an even poorer agricultural base and with many immediate problems that commanded the atttention of Mujib's quite inefficient government. Under Zia, the government accomplished much more in the rural areas in both social and agricultural work. Mujib had proposed dredging the rivers to lessen flooding, a practical approach that was not widely implemented. Zia introduced a "food for work" program that tackled smaller works, many of them irrigation projects that increased cropping intensity. This approach was somewhat more successful. It helped alleviate the serious problem of unemployment and underemployment of the landless and ease their shortage of food.

To gain the most from new strains of rice, the necessary resources must be made available on a tight schedule. The first need is seeds. Much research subsidiary to the basic research at the International Rice Research Institute in the Philippines has been undertaken in Bangladesh by the Ministry of Agriculture and other organizations. Bangladesh is using its substantial reserves of natural gas to provide nitrogenous fertilizers to supplement the animal fertilizers that have been used for centuries. The soil is generally rich, being replenished by the annual floods, but the new seeds require more than this. According to the 1977 census,[2] 51 percent of landholders used chemical fertilizers, treating 29 percent of the land. The variation between different sizes of holdings was small, although the smaller landholders treated a slightly higher percentage of their area. Along with timely irrigation, flood control is important; the water requirement involves a careful balance between too much and too little, and timing is also critical. To purchase seeds and fertilizer, farmers need credit on terms more reasonable than those of the village moneylenders. Storage, transportation, and market facilities must be vastly improved.

Another area addressed by the Ershad regime is price incentives. Governments understandably wish to provide urban populations with a standard amount of grain at reasonable prices to avoid the danger of food riots. The Bangladesh government has fixed the rice price as an added compensation to government employees and urban dwellers in Dhaka, Chittagong, and Khulna. The urban population began to see the fixed price as a permanent benefit, but it decreased the farmers' income, lessening incentives to produce a larger crop. The finance minister in the Ershad regime, A.M.A. Muhith, who has had wide experience in planning and in utilizing international assistance, heeded the long-standing demand of international lenders to terminate the ration system and the reduced prices. He acted shortly after Ershad took over, taking advantage of the absence of parliament—which would likely have defeated or watered down the proposal—and of martial law, which limited demonstrations against the action. As most of the rice entering trade channels is purchased by the government, setting the purchase price is a major tool for creating incentives.

The production of rice in Bangladesh has increased considerably since independence.[3] It took until the 1973–1974 crop year to reach the preindependence level of over 10 million tons. In 1982–1983, total output exceeded 15 million tons. Increase in yields and a slight expansion of the area under cultivation account for the increase. In 1980–1981, the area under rice cultivation was 4 percent larger than it had been ten years earlier, and the yield had increased 19.7 percent. The higher yield can be attributed to better seeds, better use of water resources, more intensive cultivation, and greater application of chemical fertilizers. There was little increase in yield during the Mujib period, but Zia's self-help program (continued under Ershad) appears to be paying off. Nonetheless, the per capita production of rice remains low, less than one pound per person per day, assuming constant availability throughout the country and the year. Bangladesh thus continues to import large quantities of food grains, both rice and wheat, to meet current demand and to build up stocks against the vagaries of the weather and the transportation system. Much of the imports comes as grant assistance from major growers such as the United States, Canada, and Australia, or through international programs financed by the Common Market countries and others, but some imports, especially rice, are purchased on the open market, at considerable cost to Bangladesh's limited foreign exchange.

Rice is not the only crop of importance to Bangladesh. Much dietary protein is derived from pulses (lentils), but production of pulses has dropped since independence: The acreage has declined somewhat (11 percent) and yield is off substantially (24 percent). Production of meat and poultry has increased by about 17 percent; that of fish, traditionally an important part of the Bengali diet, has declined by about 15 percent. When these total production figures are converted to per capita amounts for 1980–1981, rice production has increased about 15 percent since 1972, while meat and poultry has declined 3 percent and fish, 30 percent. (These figures are calculated on a 21 percent increase in population from 1972–1973 to 1980–1981, which is probably understated.)[4] It is evident that the protein content of Bangladeshi food intake is decreasing. Production has also dropped for oil seeds and for the category of condiments and spices, which includes chilis, onions, and garlic, all essential ingredients of the Bangladeshi diet.

In the international market the most important crop is jute, a fiber used to make burlap sacking, carpet backing, and rope. As noted earlier, eastern Bengal was a supplier of raw jute for Calcutta jute manufacturing mills as well as for export. After Pakistani independence in 1947, the region that is now Bangladesh began to develop its own jute manufacturing capacity, mainly with capital from West Pakistan. Jute production, subject like rice to weather conditions, has declined since Bangladeshi independence in 1971, but world demand has also declined as plastics and synthetic fibers eat into the market for jute. Overall exports have dropped about 10 percent since 1969–1970.

In a World Bank survey prepared during Zia's regime, the section on industry begins: "Rapid industrial growth is a necessary condition for the eventual solution of Bangladesh's problems of slow GDP growth, mass poverty and heavy dependence on foreign investment resources."[5] Mujib's commitment to socialism resulted in the transfer of about 85 percent of all industry to the public sector. All jute, cotton textile, and sugar factories were nationalized, and property left behind by fleeing Pakistanis was also managed by the government. Entrepreneurial talent, extremely scarce after independence, was concentrated in the private sector and not in the government. Only small—often cottage—industry was permitted in the private sector. The government enterprises were organized as a series of public corporations, whose common thread became inefficiency, overemployment, underproductivity, and regular losses. Such domestic talent and capital as was available often left the country. Mujib's socialist philosophy (although moderated markedly by successors), the real or suspected instability of the political system, and the lack of exploitable resources and labor kept foreign investors away. Bangladesh, with its small industrial base, seemed an unlikely candidate for any significant industrial expansion.

The situation in 1984 is somewhat—but only somewhat—better. Tight restrictions on foreign investment have been loosened, but the basic concerns about political instability and inadequate natural and human resources remain. The level of domestic investment has greatly increased, so that a wider range of potential industries is now available to Bangladeshi entrepreneurs. Extensive denationalization has returned property to original Bangladeshi owners, and some property has also been sold off. The lack of a legal agreement between Pakistan and Bangladesh on evacuee property has restricted divestiture of units formerly owned by West Pakistanis, including the huge Adamjee Jute Mill in Narayanganj. The climate for investment thus improved during the Zia regime. The Ershad government has extended the concessions begun under Zia and has moved to denationalize some banks.

Between 1973–1974, the first year after immediately needed reconstruction was completed, and 1980–1981, industrial production rose 45 percent. The private sector grew 64 percent, but the public sector grew only 39 percent, even with electricity output more than doubling. Cotton textiles and jute manufactures, which account for more than one-fifth of public sector production, performed below average, with increases of 15 and 14 percent respectively. In the private sector, chemical and electrical equipment manufacturing showed the highest increases.

It is difficult to predict how a more liberalized investment policy will affect the low status of manufacturing. The shortage of trained labor will undoubtedly continue to be a factor. Bangladesh has lost much skilled labor to the Middle East and has lost others through the brain drain to the West. Medical personnel and other highly skilled Bangladeshi's have left, and many skilled industrial workers, who are in great demand, have gone to the Middle East. Bangladeshis with lesser skills, such as household workers, have also sought jobs elsewhere. Official remittances from foreign countries, which amounted to about $0.5 billion a year in 1982–1983, are a major contribution to the foreign exchange accounts.[6] Not all of the remittances benefit the economy: Investment in real estate has served to drive up the price of land and create more landless in districts such as Noakhali and Comilla. But as the demand for land, transistors, and refrigerators begins to level off, and if some acceptable mechanism (such as a mutual fund) is devised to channel these funds, there may be some investment advantage in the future. In the meantime, the shortage of trained personnel is only partly mitigated by the foreign remittances.

The domestic infrastructure of Bangladesh is still weak. Much needs to be done to improve its transportation systems and its communications systems in particular. (Bangladesh did join the world of international direct dialing in December 1983.) Many bridges have not been rehabilitated since the civil war, and much of the road system is interrupted by often unreliable ferries across major waterways. Natural gas and electricity are fairly plentiful on the east side of the main Ganga-Brahmaputra river system, but across the rivers, the southwest part of the country still depends on oil-fired generators. A project to join the electricity grids is under way, but extending gas service will take much longer and will be very costly, if indeed it is feasible from the engineering point of view. Gas is one of the country's most important resources, used for domestic and industrial purposes, electricity, and chemical manufacturing, but the development of liquid natural gas for export is years away.

Bangladesh's export trade is based on traditional items, especially jute and tea. Exports of tea, grown in the highlands of Sylhet District, have been fairly steady. Volume (5.8 percent of exports in 1980–1981) is unlikely to increase greatly, however, as Bangladeshi tea ranks below that of India and Sri Lanka in quality. Jute and jute products account for by far the greatest share of exports—69 percent. Exports of another traditional product, leather and skins (8.5 percent), might be expanded somewhat. Shrimp has been added to traditional fish exports, and together fish and shellfish make up 7.5 percent of export trade.[7] Expansion of nontraditional areas will not be an easy task.

The largest customer for Bangladeshi exports has been the United States (12.4 percent of exports in 1979–1980). Collectively, the European Common Market nations took 20.5 percent. Others with substantial imports from Bangladesh were Pakistan (7.5 percent), the Soviet Union (6.4 percent), Iran (6.2 percent), Japan (4.7 percent), and China (4.3 percent). The large amount for Pakistan shows the closer relationship that has developed between the former partners during and after the Zia period. Although Bangladesh was the leader in founding the new South Asian Regional Council (SARC, recently renamed the South Asian Regional Cooperation), only a small amount of exports are taken by members other than Pakistan: India takes 1 percent and Sri Lanka and Nepal even less. Altogether, SARC accounts for 9 percent of Bangladesh's exports.

Bangladesh has had unfavorable balances of trade and payments continuously since independence. The trade balance, favorable in all but two years prior to 1969, has deteriorated since then, amounting to a deficit of nearly $10 billion in 1980–1981. Much of the deficit has been offset by foreign economic assistance. New commitments by foreign donors in 1980–1981 amounted to $1.6 billion, of which about $600 million was grant money. Although grants make up a more significant portion of its assistance, Bangladesh, like other Third World nations, faces a major debt servicing and repayment problem. Some loans may be converted to grants, but others will require payment, and exports are unlikely to furnish sufficient funds. U.S. assistance includes food grants under PL 480 and also grants for development, primarily in the rural areas. These grant programs go beyond simple agricultural development to the important areas of population planning and health delivery.

Bangladesh has applied to the International Monetary Fund (IMF) for relief, but the IMF places strict requirements on the potential borrower. The IMF curtailed an extended fund facility in 1981 but did grant Bangladesh a limited compensatory fund facility in February 1982. The IMF requirements for administrative and fiscal reforms make eminent good sense for a nation higher on the development scale but are unwarranted for a country with the difficulties Bangladesh faces. It seems evident that Bangladesh will achieve neither a balanced budget nor a positive balance of trade in the foreseeable future. Foreign assistance, whether from the IMF or other donors, is a very long term prospect for Bangladesh. Requirements to qualify for assistance must be compatible with the reasonable capabilities of the Bangladeshi government.

SOCIAL ISSUES

Population Growth

Bangladesh faces no greater problem than its ever-increasing population. Any increase in the standard of living depends upon controlling this growth, and this may apply to political stability as well. Despite efforts by the successive governments of Pakistan and Bangladesh, the annual rate of growth from 1961 to 1981 was 2.59 percent; in that period the population reportedly grew by 71.2 percent from 50.8 million to 87.1 million, and both figures are probably too low. Although the rate has supposedly declined to about 2.3 percent, even that pace means a doubling of the population in about thirty years, assuming no Malthusian events—disease, famine, or war— intervene.

The reports of experts who have studied the population problem in Bangladesh would fill a moderately sized library. Every conceivable device and incentive seems to have been tried to induce people to limit the size of their families, but the traditional attachment to having large numbers of children persists, especially among the men. Bangladeshis argue that the high infant mortality rate requires many births to ensure that some children will survive. On farms, many hands are needed to do the required work. Parents expect their children to serve as a social security system when they are old and unable to work. Sons are needed because daughters leave the family of birth for the family of marriage. The pleas for birth control, which seem so practical to outsiders, are generally ignored, except possibly the toll of numerous children on the mother's health. One means of taking the message of family planning to the rural and poorer urban areas is to appeal to the women rather than the men, who often see many children as a sign of virility. This approach has not yet developed to the point where large-scale appraisal is possible.

Substantial foreign and international organization assistance has been given to Bangladesh to help in meeting family planning goals. The United States, which for many years avoided such programs, has been involved almost since independence, as have several Scandinavian agencies and both United Nations and private organizations. Upper income–level Bangladeshis are largely convinced of the need to limit families, but most lower-income urban and rural families are not. Opposition from Muslim religious leaders has been minimal. Opposition to family planning appears to be largely male. Short of stringent rules placed by the government, which might well have dire political consequences, education and propaganda are the only routes available. These are primarily targeted at women rather than men.

Education

Related to the population problem is the problem of developing the educational system. Literacy is extraordinarily low in Bangladesh, about 20 percent, even measured by standards that fall below functional literacy. The government maintains that 60 percent of eligible students are attending primary school, but this figure may include those who attended at some time during the school year. A visit to a Bangladeshi village will confirm that at critical agricultural periods most children are not in school. It is difficult to convey the message of development or family planning to a population that is barely literate at best. Female literacy and school attendance are significantly lower than male levels, compounding the difficulty of targeting women for family planning education.

Among the different types and levels of schools, official figures for 1981–1982 state that 75.8 percent (a bit more than 8 million) of all attending students (almost 11 million) are enrolled in primary schools. Another 3.6 percent attend Islamic schools (madrassas), which are largely substandard in modern terms. About 2.5 percent attend degree-granting institutions (colleges, universities, higher technical schools, or postgraduate and professional schools). The majority of advanced students are in academic departments that, although perhaps culturally useful, are not development-oriented. Yet the Second Five Year Plan allocates only 41 percent of funds to primary education and another 9.4 percent to mass (i.e., adult) literacy. This seems indeed to be putting the cart before the horse. In annual terms, the total budget for education—current and development—is but 1.37 percent of the 1982–1983 overall budget, and even in current terms this amounts to about a dollar and a half per capita; in constant terms it may be as little as fifty cents. The resources of Bangladesh are minimal, and little foreign assistance is aimed specifically at literacy and primary education programs, except for some funds from the Middle East directed at madrassa education.

In the social setting of Bangladesh, education is largely directed at males, although at the higher levels the discrepancy is smaller. Women make up about 20 percent of the student body in colleges and universities. At the more important level of primary education, this proportion is much smaller. The common practice of purdah (seclusion of women) among Muslims hides the contributions of rural women to the economy. Many manage the farms, prepare the seed, process the crop, working indoors or in the family homestead area. At the higher income levels, many Bangladeshi women are active in occupations, such as teaching and medicine, considered "proper" for females. Others have branched out into new professions such as law and business, although not without criticism from self-appointed keepers of the national conscience. However, the very few women involved in nontraditional occupations serve to highlight the wasting of a national asset.

Health

In Bangladesh, health services are minimal and disease is pandemic. Even in the urban areas, government hospitals as well as most privately operated hospitals are well below international standards; perhaps the best-run hospital in Bangladesh is operated by U.S. medical missionaries in Chittagong District. The competence of physicians is frequently high, but many doctors have left for jobs overseas, and poor nursing, sanitation, and administrative services often negate the quality care of the remaining physicians and surgeons. In the rural areas, the shortage of medical personnel is severe. In 1981, the ratio of doctors in Bangladesh was about 1 to every 9,500 people; registered nurses, about 1 to 25,000; and hospital beds, about 1 to 4,000. The professional personnel are supplemented by midwives, pharmacists, local technicians (often poorly trained) and health visitors, whose work usually includes not only health problems as such but also family planning activities.

Almost all tropical diseases, except yellow fever, are present in Bangladesh, including malaria, cholera, and also a wide variety of intestinal diseases that are difficult to treat or eradicate. Malaria has been especially difficult to eradicate in a country where stagnant water is almost everywhere. On the other hand, great strides in the treatment of cholera have been made in Dhaka at the former SEATO (Southeast Asia Treaty Organization) Cholera Research Laboratory, now an international laboratory and hospital for the study of this disease and others affecting the intestinal tract. Nearly thirty years of intensive study of one area, Matlab in Comilla District, has provided invaluable data for a wide range of health, family planning, and educational indicators. The institute maintained a close relationship with the Johns Hopkins University for many years.

Many of the endemic diseases are water-borne, yet very few locations have safe drinking water systems. Continuing efforts to provide safe water have been made with international assistance since before independence, but maintaining a system is difficult, especially with the need for constant pressure in the lines to prevent contamination by groundwater. Improvements have been made in Chittagong and Khulna, but most educated Bangladeshis and foreigners boil water before using it. An adequate solution to the sanitation problem also lies far in the future.

Urbanization

Problems of health and sanitation are magnified for urban dwellers, still a small portion of Bangladesh's mostly rural population.

PHOTO 7.2 Village women drawing water from a well. (Courtesy of Rudolph von Bernuth)

In 1891, barely 2 percent of the people lived in urban areas; by 1961, the number had reached just over 5 percent. Since then, urbanization has proceeded more rapidly: Urban dwellers accounted for almost 9 percent of the population in 1974, and 10.6 percent in 1981, as the rate tapered off. Only Dhaka (35.9 percent), Chittagong (25.9 percent), and Khulna (17.2 percent) districts are above the national average, showing the importance of the three largest cities. Urbanization has been caused largely by two factors: the possibility of employment in the cities and the lack of opportunity in the rural areas. Unfortunately, the two do not mesh. The population has expanded more rapidly than employment opportunities. One result is serious under- or unemployment in the rural areas; another is higher unemployment in urban areas. Many who leave the rural areas have few or no skills, and the necessary resources are not available for retraining. Nonetheless, these migrants must be cared for: They need food and medical care, and their children need to be educated. This puts a large strain on municipal operations, although, of course, much the same facilities would be required had the migrants remained in the rural areas.

The urbanization of a growing number of unemployed, undernourished, and ill-housed people can pose a potential political problem. Organizing a discontented rural population appears to be a hard task in Bangladesh, but the congregation of so many in three major cities could make the task much easier. The government is aware of this and has taken steps to ameliorate conditions in urban areas. One program was the former food rationing plan, under which government employees and some others received food (mainly grains) at reduced prices.

Religion

Relations between the religious communities of Bangladesh have generally been harmonious since independence. Both the Awami League and the Bangladesh Nationalist Party have included Hindu and other non-Muslim members. The cabinet of Mujib included two prominent Hindus, and the early cabinets of Zia also included non-Muslims. The Hindu minority, as noted, has decreased substantially since independence, especially in the period between 1951 and 1961, and the Hindu population dropped again after the war of independence. In 1961, the percentage of Hindus was reported to be 18.5 percent; this had dropped to 13.5 percent by 1974. The proportion between higher-caste and Scheduled Caste Hindus has also changed. In 1961, 50.9 percent of the Hindus were high caste; by 1974 the percentage had declined to 46.8. The better educational opportunities for higher caste Hindus and their family ties in West Bengal no doubt encouraged many who left during the civil war to remain behind in Calcutta and elsewhere rather than return to Bangladesh. The Indian government complains about illegal immigrants, but most are Muslims looking for work, not Hindus seeking safety.

Zia altered the constitution of Bangladesh during his rule to dilute the secular provisions established by Mujib. He modified the document to give a moderate primacy to Islam but at the same time attempted to assure non-Muslims that their opportunities would not be curtailed. The change was made principally to accommodate the demands of Middle Eastern countries, especially Saudi Arabia, that a recipient of Islamic economic assistance should be properly Islamic. Zia may also have feared a rising Islamic fundamentalism in Bangladesh, a danger that failed to materialize, as Bengali Islam remains a personal and not a political matter. Zia was so concerned about making the change that he called minority leaders to the presidential residence to reassure them the day before the amendment was announced.

Christians comprised about 0.3 percent of the Bangladeshi population in 1974, and about the same share in 1961. The role of Christian missions in health and education has already been mentioned. There seems to be little conversion except within and among denominations of Christians and little fear among Christians for their welfare. The missions require assistance from overseas, and on several occasions conservative and Islamic elements of the government have tried to curtail this funding. There are specific rules for how funds may be transmitted, and interpreting these rules is a source of difficulty. However, Bangladesh recognizes that much of the international support it received in 1971 came from mission groups in the United States and the West, and the government does not wish to lose this constituency.

Culture

Culturally, Bangladesh remains a mixed nation. It continues to honor its rich past, which is both Hindu and Muslim. Tagore is perhaps the only poet to have composed the words for the national anthems of two states, India and Bangladesh. His songs occupy first place for all Bengalis, and a wide range of poets of both religions have succeeded him. Nazrul Islam, who lived in Calcutta with a Hindu wife, is perhaps the most highly regarded of the Muslim writers; others, including Jasimuddin, are also highly esteemed. Calcutta continues to draw the older Bangladeshi artists, but a new school for writers in all forms and for the arts is developing in Dhaka. Films are an important area of development, although they are often modelled on Indian prototypes. Bangladeshis have produced films of quality as well as some keyed to the masses rather than to the intellectual elite.

The publishing industry is not strong. The number of books published, in Bengali or English, is well below the per capita production in India and somewhat below Pakistan's production. Most writers of scholarly material seek publishers in the West or in India. Bangladeshi fiction in its various forms is still in the developing stage, but the prospect of increasing the production of fiction books is great.

The newspaper industry is at best mixed. The largest newspaper, *Ittefaq*, was founded by a noted political journalist and is carried on by his son. It has been suppressed by both the Ayub and Mujib regimes for constantly calling for a free society. The largest English newspaper, the *Bangladesh Observer* (formerly the *Pakistan Observer*), was taken over by the government after independence because its owner, Hamidul Haq Chaudhury, a lawyer and former foreign minister, had remained behind in Pakistan. The government has recently returned the newspaper to him, and the level of journalism may improve. The *People*, an Awami League daily, has ceased publication, and the *Bangladesh Times*, a government daily, is a poor substitute. Other Bengali dailies and weeklies generally espouse a particular point of view and must be read in that context.

In the social and cultural areas, Bangladesh presents the picture of a nation moving slowly but deliberately toward free expression, a movement that unfortunately has been interrupted by frequent resort to martial law.[8]

NOTES

1. Unless otherwise stated in the text or in a footnote, data in this and the following section are taken from or developed from the *Statistical Yearbook of Bangladesh, 1981*, published by the Ministry of Planning, Dacca.

2. Data in this paragraph are developed from the 1977 agricultural census and from information contained in F. Thomasson Jannuzi and James T. Peach, *The Agrarian Structure of Bangladesh: An Impediment to Development* (Boulder, Colo.: Westview Press, 1980).

3. Data in the *Statistical Yearbook of Bangladesh, 1981*, have been supplemented by reports in the *Bangladesh News*, published periodically by the Embassy of Bangladesh, Washington, D.C.

4. *Statistical Yearbook of Bangladesh, 1981*.

5. *Bangladesh: Current Trends and Development Issues* (Washington, D.C.: International Bank for Reconstruction and Development, March 1979), p. 41.

6. This is an unofficial estimate by a Bangladeshi government official for the 1983–1984 financial year.

7. Data in this section and in the rest of this chapter are taken from or derived from the *Statistical Yearbook of Bangladesh, 1981*.

8. Little has been published on the cultural development of Bangladesh. See bibliography under "Arts and Culture" for what little material exists on the subject.

8

Bangladesh in the World System

Not surprisingly, Bangladesh's most important relations in the international system are with India. Neither Bangladesh nor Pakistan can ignore their large neighbor or the effect of its size, views, and actions on the domestic and international activities of the younger nations. Bangladesh must base its foreign policy upon its geopolitical situation. Recognizing this, Bangladesh under Zia took the lead among South Asian nations in forming the South Asian Regional Cooperation system, crystallized by a formal agreement of the countries' foreign ministers in August 1983.

BANGLADESH AT INDEPENDENCE

Burdened by economic and social problems, Bangladesh entered the world system in 1971 unrecognized by most countries and, in effect, unwanted by the United Nations. Despite near unanimous popular condemnation of the brutal suppression of the East Pakistanis by the Pakistani military, all of the democratic nations of the West voted alongside Pakistan when Pakistan took its case to the Security Council and the General Assembly in December 1970. There was no question that Indian forces had invaded Pakistani land, that the Indians were aiding and abetting a secessionist movement (and had been doing so before the actual boundary crossing), and that the Indian action was against the principles of the United Nations Charter, however great the oppression by the national government of Pakistan. Only India, its Soviet ally, and the satellites and clients of the USSR voted against Pakistan, and the Soviet veto killed two resolutions in the Security Council. A resolution calling for a cease-fire and Indian withdrawal passed by a large majority in the General Assembly, but it lacked the status of a council resolution. In part, the vote expressed a refusal to recognize that united Pakistan was dead and that unwonted suffering in Bangladesh had been cut short by the Indian action. However, a more important consideration was that almost every nation has a dissident and potentially separatist group within its borders. Approving the Indian action would set a precedent for states to intervene in the domestic disputes of their neighbors. Therefore, the birth of Bangladesh as a nation met with international disapproval.

Recognition came slowly. India and Bhutan acted quickly, as did the Soviet Union and its satellites. Pakistan instituted its version of the West German Hallstein Doctrine of the 1950s, announcing that it would break diplomatic relations with any state that recognized Bangladesh, but it soon abandoned this policy when the United Kingdom, France, Germany, and Japan accorded recognition. Pakistan did withdraw from the Commonwealth when Bangladesh was admitted—and has spent some of its energy under Ziaul Haq trying to be readmitted over Indian objections. The holdouts were the United States, the People's Republic of China (PRC), and most of the Arab and Islamic states with which Pakistan had a close relationship.

The United States maintained its consulate general in Dhaka and from there directed its growing relief assistance. Under pressure from the Bangladeshis, Washington belatedly raised its mission to an embassy in April 1972 and tried to reverse the bad feelings that the ill-advised Nixon-Kissinger policy during 1971 had created in Dhaka. In addition to opposing open Indian assistance to the freedom fighters, the United States had moved a carrier task force into the Bay of Bengal in December 1971.

In February 1974, Prime Minister Bhutto of Pakistan hosted a meeting of the heads of Islamic states in Lahore. The secretary-general of the meeting had invited Mujib, but he refused to attend unless Pakistan recognized Bangladesh. Many nations noted the absence of Bangladesh, one of the largest of that group. Several Arab leaders took the initiative, persuaded Bhutto to extend an invitation, and a delegation flew to Dhaka to bring Mujib back with them. The invitation conveyed de facto recognition by Pakistan and by the Arab and Islamic states, although the exchange of ambassadors with all of these nations was not completed until after Zia took power.

The PRC, which had supported a united Pakistan in the United Nations, did not change its stance until after the 1975 coup against Mujib, when it established diplomatic relations with the Mushtaque government. At Pakistan's request, the PRC had also used its veto in the Security Council to block Bangladeshi admission to the United

Nations. Bangladesh was finally admitted to the UN in 1974. Bangladesh has chosen not to have relations with Israel and South Africa but now has relations with all other states with which diplomatic contact is deemed necessary. There are forty Bangladeshi embassies abroad, some with more than a single accreditation, and sixty-nine states have embassies in Dhaka, although not all with resident ambassadors.

REGIONAL RELATIONSHIPS

Almost all of Bangladesh's land boundary is with India; the small remainder borders on Burma in the extreme southeastern corner. The key issue in the relationship with India is water, the blessing and curse of Bangladesh. Almost all the country's water flows through India before entering Bangladesh.

It was on the issue of water, specifically Farakka Barrage, that the honeymoon between India and Bangladesh, Indira Gandhi and Mujibur Rahman, foundered, although other issues were present as well. India had been slow in withdrawing from Bangladesh, and when it did it took almost all of the Pakistani military equipment left behind by the defeated army and also transferred prisoners of war to India. This, along with India's failure to include Bangladeshis in the surrender ceremony, left a particularly bad taste among the military. Further, even as they withdrew from the plains of Bangladesh, the Indians hung on longer in the strategic Chittagong Hill Tracts for reasons not appreciated by the Bangladeshis. In the past, Pakistan had used this area as a base from which to assist tribal groups in India, such as the Mizos, who were opposed to the central government. India wanted to forestall any such use of the area by the Bangladeshis— highly unlikely in any case. In March 1972, the Indians completed their withdrawal.

As East Bengalis, many who were now Bangladeshi had supported separation from India in 1947, and they still wished to avoid domination by their larger neighbor. When Mujib contracted a treaty with India, these people opposed it. The twenty-five year agreement of March 1972 was labeled a Treaty of Friendship, Cooperation, and Peace. Some saw it as a commitment by Mujib to accept Indian claims to predominance in the subcontinent, especially as its principal rival, Pakistan, had been divided. The treaty and consultations between the two countries did identify a number of problems between them. Among these were the demarcation of the land boundary and the settlement of problems caused by enclaves, the water problem created by the Indian implementation of the long-standing project at Farakka, the sea boundary, the repatriation of Bangladeshis who had fled during 1971, and assistance and trade relationships. After the fall of Mujib another topic would be added: the support given by India to Mujib partisans operating against Zia. Still another issue is the migration of Bangladeshis, both before and after independence, into India, especially Assam.

In May 1974, the two countries signed an agreement to settle the land-border question. A long-standing agreement between India and Pakistan had decreed the exchange of enclaves through relocating people and redrawing boundaries, but this was thwarted by the opposition of the government of West Bengal, without whose approval the boundaries could not be changed. The 1974 pact retained the existing border but arranged for free transit from Bangladesh to its enclaves. There have been numerous problems in implementation, but neither side has abrogated the agreement. More recently, an important border problem has arisen between Bangladesh and Assam. Widespread and often violent agitation in Assam against "illegal immigrants," i.e., Muslims moving in from East Pakistan and then Bangladesh, had for some time prevented the continuation of representative government in that state. There is little doubt that over the years Bangladeshis have crossed the border for economic reasons, and this migration continues today. Many have managed to regularize their status and have been voting and performing other acts as citizens of India. The most recent suggestion of the Assamese government, which has apparently been approved by New Delhi, is to erect a fence along the border to check the migration. Bangladesh has bitterly protested this "unneighborly" act, meanwhile proposing to take all steps possible to stop the migration it denies exists. India has also been concerned about migration in smaller numbers into West Bengal, which echoes the pattern existing before 1947 when labor from the eastern areas supported the industries and the port of the Calcutta area. As mentioned earlier, many Hindus from East Pakistan did not return from their 1971 exile and remain in India.

The sea matter is tied into a Bangladeshi proposal to the Law of the Sea Conference that the base line for determining the sovereign area and the economic zone be calculated on the basis of the mean low water mark, not the mean high water mark. This would push the Bangladeshi boundary a significant distance into the Bay of Bengal. Bangladesh is at the end of a large indentation in the sea, and its economic zone is therefore limited by both India and Burma. The already-discovered gas areas close to shore raise the hope that more gas and oil lie under the sea and would be of benefit to the poor nation. Bangladesh has gained no support for its position. Further, it has been unable to reach agreement with India on the sea boundary for the sovereign area and the economic zone between the two countries. The issue was complicated in the late 1970s by the appearance of a new island almost squarely on the prospective boundary. Both countries claimed the new island, and sent naval landing parties. A military confrontation was barely averted, but talks have not yet settled the issue.

The key area of disagreement between the two countries, however, is Farakka and the broader issue of water rights. A joint rivers commission was set up as part of the 1972 treaty, and when the Farakka Barrage was opened in 1975 an interim agreement assured Bangladesh a minimum amount of water during the low-flow period of April and May. As a permanent solution, India supports the construction of a link canal to carry the waters of the Brahmaputra to the Ganges. This canal would begin just upstream of the border and traverse mainly Bangladeshi territory to reach an outflow just upstream from the barrage. Although feasible from an engineering point of view, the project would be very costly and would also require that a large number of residents of northwestern Bangladesh be displaced and resettled. The canal would curtail the high flood flow of the Brahmaputra and ensure adequate water for both the Calcutta project and the irrigation of southwestern Bangladesh. Bangladesh has proposed a tripartite discussion and agreement that would include Nepal, which could harness and store the tributary water to generate hydroelectric power. India has refused to "internationalize" what it regards as a bilateral issue. In 1977, with the Janata Party in power in India and Zia ruling in Bangladesh, the two governments reached a new agreement that allocated the waters in the low-flow period on a compromise basis for the next five years, during which the states were to reach a permanent arrangement. They failed to do so. Negotiations continue in the 1980s with a Gandhi government back in New Delhi. The negotiating team in Dhaka is now led by Minister of Agriculture and Irrigation Obaidullah Khan. Communiqués from a series of meetings do not give hope for an early agreement, but the fruitless and repetitive discussions of the past may be over.

Relations with Pakistan developed apace once the initial shock of the loss of the east wing wore off in Pakistan and the thorny problem of the prisoners of war was settled. The first step in solving the problem—the July 1972 agreement between Gandhi and Bhutto at Simla—did not directly involve the government of Bangladesh.

India continued to represent Bangladesh in the discussions that followed, but it was not until after the February 1974 Islamic summit meeting in Lahore that major progress was made. In April, representatives of all three governments met in New Delhi and worked out a final settlement of both the civilian-detainee and prisoner-of-war issues. Mujib dropped his claim to try 195 prisoners as war criminals, and Pakistan expressed its "regret" for "any crimes" that may have been committed. Bhutto paid a state visit to Dhaka in June, but he and Mujib did not reach agreement on establishing diplomatic relations. The exchanges of prisoners and detainees went forward as planned, and with assistance from the United Nations high commissioner for refugees, Bangladesh began sending Biharis to Pakistan. In early 1975, the two states agreed on the division of the external debt of united Pakistan, but the question of how to split the assets is still unresolved. Diplomatic relations were established in 1976, after Mujib had left the scene.

As united Pakistan, the two countries of Pakistan and Bangladesh had sought independence from India in 1947 because they were concerned about the progress and security of Muslims in a Hindu majority state. As separate countries, they continue to share a community of interests in limiting the dominance of India as well as a common Islamic position. Bangladesh's views on the Afghanistan issue are very close to those of Pakistan. Dhaka is moderately cool toward the Soviet Union and relatively close to China and the United States, positions that differ only in degree from those of Islamabad. Trade between the two former partners has increased; banks and commercial offices have opened; and travel is relatively free. Future Pakistani investment in Bangladesh is a possibility, as is the restoration of former Pakistani assets, although this will take major compromises.

President Zia was the first South Asian head of government since 1971 to visit all of the other major South Asian nations: India, Pakistan, Nepal, and Sri Lanka. He visited Sri Lanka during a meeting of the nonaligned movement, but made specific and serial visits to the other three. Zia preached to Bangladesh's neighbors his proposal for regional cooperation between the seven countries of the area (including the Maldives and Bhutan). Pakistan initially opposed this proposal because it feared India would dominate the group, and India was also doubtful, perhaps because it saw the plan as a means to limit its domination. Zia made a formal proposal in August 1980. A series of meetings by the seven foreign ministers culminated in a formal agreement in New Delhi in August 1983 establishing the South Asian Regional Cooperation. The group avoids political matters and strictly bilateral issues but has agreed to explore a wide range of social, economic, environmental, and technological issues. It is a far cry from a common market, which has been suggested by some individuals, but the group is a promising start toward restoring a level of cooperation that has been absent since the British left.

Bangladesh has close relations with the South Asian nations it shares common issues with, but there is little trade between Bangladesh and the other SARC nations. Nepal and Bhutan have looked for a possible alternative port in Chittagong and Khulna (the port of Chalna). Nepal has also given some indication of its willingness to join the Ganges talks between India and Bangladesh.

Burma is not usually considered part of South Asia, although it belonged to the British Indian Empire until 1937. Relations between Bangladesh and Burma have generally been cordial, with the exception of a strange and, happily, short-lived incident in 1978. After their government refused to issue them citizen identity cards, perhaps as many as 200,000 Arakanese Muslims fled across the Burmese border into Chittagong District. The Bangladesh government gave assistance to the Muslim refugees, who arrived in a wet and already crowded area. Careful negotiations by the Zia government resulted in the return of the refugees to the Arakan area in Burma and the restoration of better relations between the two countries.

THE ISLAMIC STATES

Despite Pakistan's pressure against recognition of Bangladesh, especially by fellow Muslim-majority states, it was inevitable that many would soon establish some relationship with one of the four largest Muslim states in the world (Indonesia is first and there are nearly equal numbers in Bangladesh, Pakistan, and India). As noted above, the Lahore Islamic summit in February 1974 broke the final barriers to recognition.

For the more conservative Islamic states an additional drawback was that Bangladesh had proclaimed itself a secular and not an Islamic state. These states, notably Saudi Arabia, therefore delayed recognition until after the murder of Mujib, when it seemed the secular orientation of Mujibism might be modified. Recognition came with the advent of the Mushtaque government, although Zia was in office before a Saudi ambassador arrived. At present, Bangladesh has resident ambassadors from and in almost all of the Arab League countries as well as Iran, Turkey, Pakistan, Indonesia, and Malaysia.

PHOTO 8.1 Sher-i-Bangla Nagar (named for Fazlul Huq), Dhaka. The modern building in the area once called Ayubnagar (after Ayub Khan) houses the Bangladeshi parliament when it is in session. It was used for the Islamic summit meeting in December 1973. (Courtesy of Rudolph von Bernuth)

Bangladesh needed more than recognition from the oil-rich nations. Some were hesitant to assist a nation that had not formally changed its constitutional adherence to secularism. As noted above, Zia reformulated the clause on secularism, adding the statement that in Bangladesh, Muslims would be able to order their lives in accordance with the Quran and the Sunna. The change did not create major concern among non-Muslims. After Zia's death and the coup led by Ershad, it appeared for a time that Ershad would steer Bangladesh further toward becoming an Islamic state. Several of his public statements indicated that his views were much more Islamic than those of his predecessors, including Mushtaque.[1] However, Ershad has since retreated markedly from this position, dropping several advisers who advocated greater Islamic measures, and he appears prepared to continue the moderate Zia formulation. His concern that Islamic fundamentalist groups will attain greater strength than their miniscule election returns indicate is seemingly unwarranted.[2] Islam is still much more of a personal than a state matter in Bangladesh.

In the fiscal years 1974–1975 through 1980–1981, aid commitments to Bangladesh amounted to $8.831 billion, although not nearly this much has been disbursed. Of the total funds committed, $391 million (4.4 percent) has come from the Arab nations, with $170 million (1.9 percent of the total) coming from Saudi Arabia. Saudi assistance has included $70 million in food grants, $1 million in nonproject grants, and $49 million in project grants. The remaining $50 million has been in the form of project loans.[3] The other Arab countries giving assistance are Iraq, Kuwait, and the United Arab Emirates. Rapprochement with other Muslim countries, after overcoming Pakistani objections and modifying the constitution, has thus been profitable for Bangladesh. However, 62.7 percent of the Arab assistance has been in the form of loans, adding to the already substantial debt burden of Bangladesh.

The Middle East imports much Bangladeshi labor—a mixed blessing, as already described. The Middle East also serves as a market for Bangladesh's limited nontraditional exports (small manufactures such as batteries and shoes) although Pakistan is well ahead in this field. The Arab states are Bangladesh's principal source of imported petroleum.

Bangladesh has become an important member of the Organization of the Islamic Conference; a Bangladeshi candidate for secretary-general of the group was nominated in 1983. Bangladesh was one of the appointed mediators in the organization's unsuccessful attempt to settle the war between Iran and Iraq. Bangladesh is also a member of the Al-Quds (Jerusalem) Committee, which seeks to return most of Jerusalem to Arab control through a restoration of the pre-1967 dividing line in Palestine. This would place areas sacred to Jews, Christians, and Muslims back under Muslim control. The country also took a firm stand against the Khomeini regime's position in holding U.S. hostages, and former president of Bangladesh Abu Sayeed Chaudhury, was among those proposed by the United States as a mediator. Bangladesh has also firmly opposed the Soviet invasion of Afghanistan, aligning itself with most of the Muslim nations, although it is not, like Pakistan, a front-line state.

Bangladesh has tried to stay away from intra-Arab disputes. The Zia government was embarrassed in 1977 by the Libyan embassy's attempt to enlist Bangladeshis to fight the Egyptians during one of

Qaddafi's confrontations with Sadat. A number of Bangladeshi doctors and nurses are on active duty with the Libyans.

THE GREAT POWERS

Relations between Bangladesh and the major powers—the United States, the Soviet Union, China, Japan, and Great Britain—have evolved over the twelve years since independence. With the two superpowers, the gradual changes under Mujib and more dramatic shifts under Zia and Ershad primarily reflected changing Soviet and U.S. policies toward the new state. At the time of independence, the Soviet Union was considered friendly because of its treaty with India and its welcome support in the United Nations and in the immediate aspects of rehabilitation. On the other hand, the United States government was viewed as hostile to the breakup of Pakistan; it had sent the *Enterprise* and its accompanying task force to the mouth of the Bay of Bengal and had opposed the formation of Bangladesh at the United Nations. China had taken, in the eyes of Bangladeshis, a stance similar to that of the United States. The United Kingdom, however, supported immediate Bangladeshi entry into the Commonwealth and had welcomed Mujib in London, when he stopped there unexpectedly before returning to Dhaka from Pakistan. Japan was not seen as taking any strong position about the civil war but would soon become an important contributor to rehabilitation and development.

Despite its delay in recognizing the new regime in Dhaka, the United States moved quickly to assist Bangladesh in its efforts to regain stability under Mujib. The Agency for International Development (AID) soon opened a mission in Bangladesh. In addition, a large number of U.S. (and European) voluntary agencies began programs, many of them with commodities provided under AID-operated programs. Finance Minister Tajuddin Ahmad reportedly opposed accepting assistance from the United States unless it was channeled through the World Bank or another international agency, because of his personal leftist views and also because of his anger at the official U.S. stance during the civil war. However, Ahmad was overruled by Mujib, who recognized that the urgent needs of the country dictated accepting assistance from every available source. Bangladesh retained a strong favorable constituency in the United States, both in the public and in Congress, and the administration raised little or no opposition to aid once Bangladeshi independence was a fait accompli. The delay in appointing an ambassador did not indicate U.S. unwillingness to help, nor did the United States use the burning of the

United States Information Service (USIS) Dhaka offices in 1975 as a pretext to reduce its aid efforts.

Mujib gradually overcame his reluctance to deal with the former opponent, especially as it became clear that the United States had no strategic interests or plans that might be inimical to him or to Bangladesh. Setbacks such as the USIS incident or the accusations by some leftist Awami Leaguers about improper activities by U.S. diplomats did not change the long-range improvement in relations. A reallocation of cabinet portfolios helped: Abdus Samad Azad was dropped from the cabinet in March 1973 and Tajuddin Ahmad in November 1974, for internal party reasons. Mujib met Nixon and others of the U.S. government during his visit to the United States for the United Nations session in September 1974, and the two men achieved an understanding, if not a cordial relationship. A month later, Secretary of State Henry Kissinger stopped in Dhaka to meet Mujib, and he praised Mujib's leadership. The only other cabinet member to visit was Secretary of the Treasury John Connally, who came shortly after independence. A growing unhappiness with India during the last years of the first Gandhi regime, coupled with disenchantment with the Soviets (both governments were close to the fallen Mujib), brought a warmer U.S.-Bangladeshi relationship during the Zia period. Although the two countries disagree on a number of issues, especially those concerning the Middle East, they also have similar views on many subjects, especially the Soviet occupation of Afghanistan. Zia met briefly with President Carter in 1979, under circumstances similar to the Nixon-Mujib meeting, and General Ershad paid an official visit to President Reagan in October 1983. The talks, which were not limited despite Reagan's concern with the Grenada action begun that morning, have been described by knowledgeable sources as cordial. Reagan reportedly encouraged Ershad to move quickly to restore representative government; this was shortly before Ershad's announcement that presidential and parliamentary elections would be held in 1984. Ershad's quest for U.S. investment in Bangladesh met with a mixed reaction from business executives he met in Washington, Houston, and Los Angeles.

U.S. interests in South Asia are limited, especially in Bangladesh, despite the increased attention paid to Pakistan as a result of the Soviet invasion of Afghanistan. The United States wishes to see the nations of South Asia devote their greatest attention to economic development, under political systems that represent their peoples, and settle disputes among themselves peacefully. It claims no special influence for itself and does not want any other great power to claim such a role for itself. Within this set of policy goals, U.S. efforts can only be expended substantially in the economic development sphere; the other goals are very much in the hands of the individual nations, with little U.S. input other than encouragement.

In the area of economic assistance, the United States has contributed most to food supplies through Public Law 480. For example, during Bangladesh's fiscal year 1980–1981, 55 percent ($72 million) of the total $131 million committed by the United States went for food; 27.5 percent ($36 million) went for nonproject aid and 17.5 percent ($23 million) for projects.[4] U.S. surpluses and Bangladeshi needs have coincided. In most years since independence, the United States has been the largest bilateral donor. In the first fiscal year, which ended in 1972, the United States granted 23 percent of the total assistance, the largest single donor that year, just ahead of India. In addition to food, in the 1980s the United States has been concerned primarily with rural programs, including agriculture, health delivery, and family planning.

The United States has avoided a military relationship with Bangladesh despite requests for military equipment. It was not until 1977 that a defense attaché was added to the embassy staff; the International Military Education and Training (IMET) program was begun shortly before that. This small program brings a limited number of Bangladeshi military personnel to the United States for specialized training. In civilian educational programs, the United States, Canada, Great Britain, and Australia have all failed to maintain the momentum gained when Bangladesh was East Pakistan; the USIS exchange program was smaller in 1983 than it was before 1971. This is, in the judgment of the writer, extraordinarily foolish. The current generation of Western-trained professors will soon leave the universities, and will be replaced by many trained in the Soviet Union.

The Soviet Union moved quickly into Bangladesh after independence. Its most visible project was the clearing of Chittagong harbor, a particularly important undertaking as this was the only practical point of entry for the large amount of relief materials needed. Mujib visited Moscow in February 1972 and again in February 1974. However, the Soviets lingered in Chittagong sufficiently long to raise questions about their intentions among many Bangladeshis, who foresaw that the Soviet Union might be attempting to convert the port into a Soviet base. The weak showing of two possible Soviet allies (the Communist Party of Bangladesh and the National Awami Party [the faction led by Muzaffar Ahmad]) in the 1973 election—rigged though it was—and the decline of the pro-Moscow left of the

Awami League suggested that the future of Soviet protégés through constitutional means was limited. Soviet construction of an enormous embassy compound and the flooding of the country with a large number of Soviet technicians and advisers also disconcerted many Bangladeshis.

The result of the Soviet Union's rather heavy-handed actions has been a cooling of relations between the two countries (in 1983, Ershad expelled a number of Soviet embassy personnel). Partly this has been a by-product of less cordial relations between India and Bangladesh. Limited Soviet military assistance to Bangladesh has been all but discontinued. Of the total economic assistance committed in 1980–1981, the Soviet Union accounted for only 4.4 percent ($72 million) of the total of $1,642 million. In the first year (1971–1972) it committed 5.3 percent ($27 million) of a total of $509 million.

Politically, Bangladesh has opposed the Soviet Union on two issues important to Dhaka. Bangladesh has strongly opposed the invasion of Afghanistan and also opposed the Vietnam-supported regime in Kampuchea. These stands also differ from the positions taken by India.

China took much longer than the United States to normalize relations with Bangladesh. As mentioned earlier, the PRC remained constant in its alliance with Pakistan, neither recognizing Bangladesh nor withdrawing its veto against Bangladeshi admission to the United Nations. Pakistani recognition removed the second of these barriers. The People's Republic approved Bangladeshi admission to the United Nations in September 1974. After the fall of Mujib, the two countries established diplomatic relations. China has not been a major donor of economic assistance but has done what it can do very well, sending experts and funds especially for small irrigation projects. China has supplied Bangladesh with almost its entire flyable fleet of military aircraft and has, it is understood, also supplied small amounts of other military equipment. Zia visited China in January 1977 and further extended what can aptly be described as cordial relations. Ershad has also visited Beijing.

Japan's interest in Bangladesh has increased steadily, and Japan has become an important donor and trading partner. In 1980–1981, Japan was the largest single donor of aid to Bangladesh, with 14.1 percent ($232 million) of total commitments. In trade, Japan was second only to the United States in 1979–1980, as both a source of imports and a destination for exports. Japanese companies, as well as U.S. and some European companies, have been exploring possibilities for investment but have found few opportunities. One possibility would be to develop liquified natural gas. When Bangladesh was elected to the UN Security Council in November 1978, it defeated Japan for the "Asian seat," but this has had no long-term effect on relations between the two countries. Zia has visited Japan, as has Ershad.

The United Kingdom strongly endorsed the membership of Bangladesh in the Commonwealth, as did India and other members, despite Pakistan's threat to withdraw. At the time, they probably believed the threat to be an empty one. (Since the withdrawal, India has successfully blocked Pakistan's attempts to rejoin.) Britain has also been a substantial donor of assistance over the years and has aided a number of infrastructure projects in transportation and communications that the United States shunned for policy reasons. Cultural relations have also been close through the British Council, a Crown corporation that arranges educational exchanges. Many British voluntary agencies are operating in Bangladesh, including the British equivalent of the Peace Corps. (The U.S. organization is not permitted to work, although a framework agreement was signed in 1969.) Great Britain is also Bangladesh's largest European trading partner; West Germany is second. Some British investment remains, the largest block in a slim grand total. Queen Elizabeth visited Dhaka in November 1983, en route to the Commonwealth conference in New Delhi.

Close relations with European and Commonwealth nations are based primarily on aid relationships with both official and voluntary agencies. Indeed, almost every international assistance agency operates in Bangladesh. After Britain and Germany, Bangladesh does a moderate amount of trade with Italy, but very little with France and the remaining members of the Common Market. Among the older Commonwealth nations—Canada, Australia, and New Zealand—educational exchanges by Canada and Australia add another dimension to the basic aid relationship. Nonetheless, the total number of scholarships offered by the developed English-speaking countries is miniscule in comparison to those still offered by the Soviet Union.

INTERNATIONAL ORGANIZATIONS

After the PRC withdrew its veto and Bangladesh was admitted to the United Nations, the new state quickly joined most of the UN affiliates. Its membership in some, including the World Bank, the International Monetary Fund, and the Asian Development Bank, predates its admission. Bangladesh has used international lending facilities extensively, including the International Development Association (IDA). The credits from IDA, with longer pay-back periods, grace periods, and lower interest rates, have been particularly attractive to Bangladesh, with its low international credit rating. Bangladesh's appeal to the IMF for assistance has been put on hold pending the completion of prescribed administrative and financial reforms. Some conditions have been met by the changes instituted by Finance Minister Muhith. The basic difficulty is simply that Bangladesh's resources and capacity to increase exports are severely limited, and they are unlikely to expand in the foreseeable future. Bangladesh and some other nations in similar straits (Chad, Mali) will require special consideration if their development programs are not to founder.

Bangladesh has used the UN General Assembly as an individual forum on only one occasion. In 1977, it was able to get the Farakka water dispute inscribed on the agenda over Indian objections. The assembly took note of the matter, recommending that the two countries meet to resolve the question and report back to the assembly. This and other actions, including a reference at the Mar del Plata 1976 session on water resources contributed to the discussions that led to the interim agreement already described.

Bangladesh is a member of the nonaligned movement and the Group of 77, playing an active and moderate role in each. It was selected as one of the Third World nations to attend the Cancun conference in 1981. Bangladesh was represented there by Prime Minister Shah Azizur Rahman. Membership in these groups and in the Islamic groups has projected the views of Bangladesh more prominently than might be expected considering the poverty of the country. Its voice has been respected particularly for its moderation and willingness to compromise.

NOTES

1. So far, there has been no official compilation of the statements of President Ershad. Summaries of many are available in *Bangladesh News*, an occasional publication of the Embassy of Bangladesh, Washington, D.C. Many are also carried in full or in summary in the *Daily Report* of the Foreign Broadcast Information Service.

2. For a discussion of elections in eastern Bengal (1937), East Bengal (1954), East Pakistan (1970), and Bangladesh (1973, 1978, and 1979) see Craig Baxter and M. Rashiduzzaman, "Bangladesh Votes—1978 and 1979," *Asian Survey* 21, 4 (April 1981).

3. Bangladesh, Ministry of Planning, *Statistical Yearbook of Bangladesh, 1981* (Ministry of Planning, Dacca).

4. Ibid.

9

Prospects: Hope or Despair?

By any standard, Bangladesh's future prospects cannot be described as hopeful. Although Bangladesh is neither the largest nor the poorest country in the world, it can appropriately be called the "largest, poorest" nation. Its problems resist an early or easy solution. The single most important problem is population growth. Unless the rate of growth slows markedly, no measurable progress in the low standard of living of the overwhelming majority of the population will be possible. The impracticability of large increases in food production magnifies this problem. Although Bangladesh is working to increase yields, bring more land under cultivation, and expand multiple crop cultivation, in the long run the total increase in output will be outstripped by the growing population. Herein lies the basic problem of the nation.

While these economic and social problems continue to defy solution, Bangladesh also remains politically underdeveloped. Changes are possible but perhaps unlikely. Zia was one political leader who did gradually expand participation in the political system. The opportunity for the nation to grow further through the election of 1981 was negated by the military action of 1982. The voice of the people was silenced by military officers whose main concern was apparently their own prerogatives, and not the welfare of the country.

Bangladesh is clearly a unified nation. Almost all Bangladeshis use a single language, Bengali. The great majority profess the same religion, Islam, a creed that establishes a pervasive standard of behavior for family and social realms as well as for religious matters per se. The people of Bangladesh have in common the long history of eastern Bengal and the shorter heritage of East Pakistan, with all their high and low points. Most Bangladeshis have gone through the baptism of fire that was the struggle for independence.

113

What is missing from the catalogue of national identity is a set of common goals widely accepted by the people. Zia tried to supply this with his nineteen-point program for development and self-reliance, which he preached on his travels throughout the country. He attempted, with some success, to mobilize the people into a single group aspiring to improve their own living conditions. Realistically, Zia's goals may have been impossible to achieve. Nonetheless, they served to direct the energies of many in the rural areas. This achievement seems to have dissipated under the Ershad regime. Lacking the personal talents of his predecessor, Ershad seems to many observers to preach the politics of despair, in contrast to Zia's politics of hope.

Zia's popularization of national goals expanded popular participation in government. In 1984, despite the promise of local and then national elections, many Bangladeshis feel that the military will return unless the elections go their way, repeating what could be an unending cycle of military rule with short and temporary intervals of civilian government. Bangladesh has been under military rule twice, first from the November 1975 coups until the parliamentary elections in 1979, and again since March 1981. In twelve years of independence, martial law has thus been in effect more than half of the time—and the last part of Mujib's regime and all of Mushtaque's were authoritarian. It is a dismal record.

The politicians cannot be absolved of all blame. When Mujib saw his mandate slipping, he first rigged the elections and then pulled off a constitutional coup to become an all-powerful president. When a fair election was held in 1979, the winning party split into factions, and the opposition behaved almost as badly as the East Pakistan assembly did in 1958, when an extreme breakdown in order culminated in the death of the deputy speaker. This behavior highlights a pattern that has existed since at least 1954—and some would argue even earlier. Once in power, Bangladeshi politicians are much more concerned with office and perquisites than they are with the betterment of the country—admittedly a problem in many democracies. This does not, however, excuse those in power.

Another problem of the political system is the lack of younger leaders. The long Ayub period, which hindered development of leadership in politics, was followed by the Mujib period, in which nepotism and favoritism became the rule of the day. Many of Mujib's now discredited cronies were incompetent at best and crooked at worst. In the shadow of Ayub and Mujib, few were allowed to grow politically. Today's leading politicians either gained their experience in a much earlier era or are tyros with little experience in the art of compromise so essential to political development.

Outsiders deal with two Bangladeshes. Rural and urban poverty exists for all to see, but there is also the thin upper layer of affluent Bangladeshis, with whom outsiders generally carry on negotiations and social intercourse. This group lives well and has little incentive to redistribute wealth. Many largely ignore what goes on outside of their homes and offices. Zia, who was a member of the upper level by profession if not by birth, tried to motivate this group. It is difficult to predict whether other leaders will repeat Zia's efforts, and with what success.

In some countries, the vast inequality in income distribution might spark a revolution. For the time being, revolution seems less likely in Bangladesh than, with hindsight, it did in Cuba or Ethiopia, but the danger awaits the mobilizing capabilities of a new leader. Communications difficulties notwithstanding, a new movement could successfully undertake the task of organization. The bourgeois Awami Leaguers, the once aristocratic Muslim Leaguers, and members of the newly active Bangladesh Nationalist Party could be swept away before an uprising of the socialist and Communist left or an Islamic fundamentalist group led by the ilk of Khomeini. But if civilian politicians are given another opportunity, and if their fellow upper middle class colleagues in the military (to whom many are related) are willing to allow popular participation, there is hope for Bangladesh to renew the movement toward greater production and a higher standard of living.

Bengal has often been described as the most politicized area of the subcontinent. Although many in Bangladesh appear to be tiring of the cycle of emotional campaigns followed by great letdowns, there is yet time for a charismatic and, one would hope, practical leader to step forward. For the Muslims of Bengal, each election has had such a leader crusading for a specific purpose: Fazlul Huq campaigned to improve the conditions of the peasants in 1937; Jinnah led the way toward separation from the feared domination of the Hindus in 1946; Fazlul Haq and Suhrawardy emphasized the uniqueness of East Bengal and "Bengalness" in 1954; Mujib preached liberation from the oppression of West Pakistan in 1970, and the consolidation of independence in 1973; and finally, Zia promoted self-reliance for development in 1978 and 1979. These issues have been important enough to Bangladeshis to unify them behind their leaders.

In the 1980s, one finds almost an apathetic view of government and of how the administration might alleviate desperate conditions.

Bangladeshis lack the inspiration that a charismatic leader with a strong following could provide. For the time being, the politics of despair have replaced the politics of hope. Bangladesh must regain that hope if it is to work toward solving its problems with the continued aid and sympathy of the developed nations.

Bibliography

A number of useful bibliographic works are available that cover Bangladesh. The annual *Bibliography of Asian Studies* (Ann Arbor, Mich.: Association for Asian Studies) is essential for anyone studying South Asia, as is the work by Maureen L. P. Patterson, *South Asian Civilizations: A Bibliographic Synthesis* (Chicago: University of Chicago Press, 1981). The former usually runs three or four years behind. A somewhat dated bibliographic source is the volume edited by W. Eric Gustafson, *Pakistan and Bangladesh: Bibliographic Essays in the Social Sciences* (Islamabad; Pakistan: University of Islamabad Press, 1976). The essays, which include contributions by Gustafson on economics, Craig Baxter on history, Lawrence Ziring on politics, and Peter J. Bertocci on anthropology, are interpretive rather than simply descriptive.

Current information is more difficult to obtain for Bangladesh than for some other South Asian nations, as none of the Bangladeshi newspapers publish an overseas weekly. The Bangladeshi embassy in Washington sporadically issues a newsletter, but it is rarely up to the standard of publications by many other embassies. The February issue of *Asian Survey* contains an annual review article; and the Ministry of Planning prepares an annual *Statistical Yearbook of Bangladesh*, the source of most of the statistical data contained in this book.

BENGAL BEFORE THE BRITISH

Little recent material has been published on the earlier period. One may consult the standard general histories of India, such as A. L. Basham, *The Wonder That Was India* (New York: Grove Press, 1954); and Romila Thapar, *A History of India*, Vol. 1 (Harmondsworth, Eng.: Penguin, 1972). The most noted of Bengali historians, Ramesh Chandra Majumdar, collaborated with Jadunath Sarkar to produce a two-volume history of pre-British Bengal, *History of Bengal* (Dacca: University of Dacca Press, 1943). The first volume, by Majumdar, covers the Hindu period; the second, by Sarkar, the Muslim period.

117

THE BRITISH EMPIRE IN INDIA

The rather extensive coverage of Bengal under the British includes works by British authors writing memoirs and studies in Bengal and also more recent studies by writers who have made use of the extensive archival resources in London, Calcutta, and elsewhere. Two that are especially useful for the development of nationalism (although they shortchange the Muslims) are John H. Broomfield's *Elite Conflict in a Plural Society: Twentieth Century Bengal* (Berkeley and Los Angeles: University of California Press, 1968) and Leonard A. Gordon's *Bengal: The Nationalist Movement, 1876–1940* (New York: Columbia University Press, 1974). The Muslim point of view on the partition of Bengal is covered in M.K.U. Molla, *The New Province of Eastern Bengal and Assam* (Rajshahi, Bangladesh: Institute of Bangladesh Studies, 1981). Provincial autonomy after 1937 is studied extensively in three works: Humaira Momen, *Muslim Politics in Bengal* (Dacca: Sunny House, 1972); Enayetur Rahim, *Provincial Autonomy in Bengal (1937–1943)* (Rajshahi, Bangladesh: Institute for Bangladesh Studies, 1981); and Shila Sen, *Muslim Politics in Bengal, 1937–1947* (New Delhi: Impex, 1976). I found the slim volume by Momen to be the most useful. Kamruddin Ahmad's *A Socio-Political History of Bengal* (Dacca: Zahiruddin Mahmud, 1975) is an oft-cited work that should be supplemented by more focused studies when possible. The social and religious background of Bangladesh is treated in rather pedestrian fashion by Sufia Ahmad, *Muslim Community in Bengal, 1884–1912* (Dacca: Oxford University Press, 1974); and A. K. Nazmul Karim, *The Dynamics of Bangladesh Society* (New Delhi: Vikas, 1980).

UNITED PAKISTAN

The era of Pakistani rule is covered by a number of books. Among the general works, Richard S. Wheeler's *The Politics of Pakistan: A Constitutional Quest* (Ithaca, N.Y.: Cornell University Press, 1970) is perhaps the best, along with the more chronologically focused *The Ayub Khan Era* by Lawrence Ziring (Syracuse, N.Y.: Syracuse University Press, 1971). The events leading up to separation are analyzed with different emphases in Talukder Maniruzzaman, *The Politics of Development: The Case of Pakistan, 1947–1958* (Dacca: Green Book House, 1971); Rounaq Jahan, *Pakistan: Failure in National Integration* (New York: Columbia University Press, 1972); and G. W. Choudhury, *The Last Days of United Pakistan* (Bloomington: Indiana University Press, 1974). Choudhury was a minister in the Yahya cabinet.

CIVIL WAR AND INDEPENDENCE

The events of 1971 have been covered by a number of writers, some of them participants, but each with a particular point of view. A full study of the breakup of Pakistan is yet to come. One shorter analysis of the international implications is my chapter, "Bangladesh: The Unique Successful Case," in Frederick L. Shiels, ed., *Ethnic Separatism and World Politics* (Washington, D.C.: University Press of America, 1984). Recommended books for initial reading include A.M.A. Muhith, *Bangladesh: Emergence of a Nation* (Dacca: Bangladesh Books International, 1978); Maudud Ahmed [Moudud Ahmad], *Bangladesh: Constitutional Quest for Autonomy* (Dacca: University Press, 1979); Mizanur Rahman Shelley, *Emergence of a New Nation in a Multipolar World: Bangladesh* (Dacca: University Press, 1979); and Muhammad Abdul Wadud Bhuiyan, *Emergence of Bangladesh and the Role of the Awami League* (New Delhi: Vikas, 1982). Muhith was posted in the Pakistani embassy in Washington when the civil war began and was appointed to Ershad's cabinet; Moudud Ahmad was an adviser to Mujib and a deputy prime minister under Zia. For a Pakistani point of view, see Hasan Askari Rizvi, *Internal Strife and External Intervention: India's Role in the Civil War in East Pakistan [Bangladesh]* (Lahore, Pakistan: Progressive Publishers, 1981).

INDEPENDENT BANGLADESH

For the postindependence period, the work of Bangladesh's leading political scientist, Talukder Maniruzzaman, is essential. His *The Bangladesh Revolution and Its Aftermath* (Dacca: Bangladesh Books International, 1980) is excellent. Also valuable is Zillur Rahman Khan, *Leadership in the Least Developed Nation: Bangladesh* (Syracuse, N.Y.: Maxwell School, 1983). Rounaq Jahan, *Bangladesh Politics: Problems and Issues* (Dacca: University Press, 1980); Marcus Franda, *Bangladesh: The First Decade* (New Delhi: South Asian Publishers, 1982); and Talukder Maniruzzaman, *Group Interests and Political Change: Studies in Bangladesh and Pakistan* (New Delhi: South Asian Publishers, 1952), are noteworthy collections of articles that cover a wide range of topics concerning the new nation of Bangladesh.

The Economy

On the Bangladeshi economy, an excellent thin volume is B.L.C. Johnson's *Bangladesh*, 2d ed. (Totowa, N.J.: Barnes and Noble, 1982). The development of Bangladesh is well covered in Just Faaland and J. R. Parkinson, *Bangladesh: Test Case of Development* (Dacca: University Press, 1976). Economic development is covered extensively in official publications of the World Bank, the International Monetary Fund, the Agency for International Development, and the Bangladesh Ministry of Planning. On the present state of Islam see Peter J. Bertocci, "Bangladesh: Composite Cultural Identity and Modernization in a Muslim-Majority State," in Philip H. Stoddard, David C. Cuthell, and Margaret W. Sullivan, eds., *Change and the Muslim World* (Syracuse, N.Y.: Syracuse University Press, 1981).

Arts and Culture

Little has been published since independence on the fine arts, architecture, literature, and the performing arts in Bangladesh. The following works, some preindependence, are suggested with the caveat that they may prove difficult to find in libraries not specializing in South Asian studies. A broad survey, which includes material on Bengal, is Percy Brown's *Indian Architecture* (Bombay, Taraporevala); the first volume, *Hindu and Buddhist Period*, was republished in 1965; the second, *Islamic Period*, in 1968. Another, more specific, work is S. M. Hasan, *A Guide to the Ancient Monuments of East Pakistan* (Dacca: Society for Pakistan Studies, 1970). Ahmad Hassan Dani's *Dacca: A Record of Its Changing Fortunes* (Dacca: Mrs. S. S. Dani, 1962) is by one of Pakistan's foremost archaeologists. For contemporary painting the Bangladesh Shilpakala Academy, Dhaka, has issued a series of publications on the work of individual Bangladeshi artists. One study of the developing cinema has been published: Alamgir Kabir, *Film in Bangladesh* (Dacca: Bangla Academy, 1979). For the fine arts in general, as well as short treatments of other subjects, the promotional publication edited by Enamul Haq, *Meet Bangladesh* (Dacca: Department of Films and Publications, Government of Bangladesh, 1979) is a useful but sketchy volume. The editor was director of the Dhaka Museum. For the field of literature, see Muhammad Enamul Haq, *Muslim Bengali Literature* (Karachi: Pakistan Publications, 1957); and Syed Ali Ashraf, *Muslim Traditions in Bengali Literature* (Karachi: Bengal Literature Society, University of Karachi, 1960). On the two writers most revered among Bangladeshis, Rabindranath Tagore and Kazi Nazrul Islam, the following biographies are valuable: Krishna Kripalani, *Rabindranath Tagore: A Biography* (New York: Oxford University Press, 1962); and Gopal Halder, *Kazi Nazrul Islam* (New Delhi: Sahitya Akademi, 1973). Folk literature is covered in Ashraf Siddiqui, *Folkloric Bangladesh: A Collection of Essays on Folk Literature of Bangladesh* (Dacca: Bangla Academy, 1976).

Abbreviations

AID	Agency for International Development (U.S.)
BAKSAL	Bangladesh Krishak Sramik Awami League (Bangladesh Peasants, Workers, and Peoples League)
BNP	Bangladesh Nationalist Party
CMLA	chief martial law administrator
CSP	Civil Service of Pakistan
GDP	gross domestic product
ICS	Indian Civil Service
IDA	International Development Association
IDBP	Industrial Development Bank of Pakistan
IMF	International Monetary Fund
IMET	International Military Education and Training
JAGODAL	Jatiyo Ganatantrik Dal (National Democratic Party)
JSD	Jatiyo Samajtantrik Party (National Socialist Party)

KPP	Krishak Praja Party (Farmers Peoples Party)
KSP	Krishak Sramik Party (Peasants and Workers Party)
PICIC	Pakistan Industrial and Commercial Investment Corporation
SARC	South Asian Regional Cooperation
USIS	United States Information Service

Index

Adamjee Jute Mill, 35–36, 42, 85
Afghania. *See* Frontier, The
Afghanistan, 13, 14, 102, 105, 107, 109
Aga Khan III, 22
Agartala conspiracy case, 44
Agency for International Development
    (AID), 106
Agriculture, 3–4, 18, 21, 34, 35, 36,
    79–86, 108, 113
Ahmad, Khondakar Mushtaque. *See*
    Mushtaque Ahmad, Khondakar
Ahmad, Moudud, 66, 67, 69
Ahmad, Muzaffar, 108
Ahmad, Tajuddin, 50, 55, 58, 59, 106,
    107
Ahmad Khan, Sir Syed, 19, 22
Ahsanuddin Chaudhury, Abul Fazal
    Muhammad. *See* Chaudhury, Abul
    Fazal Muhammad Ahsanuddin
AID. *See* Agency for International
    Development
Ajlaf, 7. *See also* Vernacular elite
Akbar (Mughal emperor), 14, 15
Ali, Chaudhury Muhammad. *See*
    Muhammad Ali, Chaudhury
Ali, Mansur. *See* Mansur Ali
Aligarh, 22
Alivardi, 15
Al-Quds (Jerusalem) Committee, 105
Ambassadors, 32, 33, 35, 98–99, 109
Amin, Nurul. *See* Nurul Amin
Aminul Islam, 69
Animists, 9
Arab League countries, 103
Arab states, 98, 105–106
Arakanese Muslims, 103
Area, 1
Ashoka (ca. 274–232 B.C.), 12
Ashraf, 7
Asian Development Bank, 110
Assam Province, 18, 24–25, 28, 37, 76,
    100

Assassinations, 39, 43, 50, 58, 59, 60,
    66–67
Ataur Rahman Khan, 41, 44, 50, 63
Aurangzeb, 14
Awami League, 11, 19, 39, 41, 42, 43,
    44, 49–53, 55, 57, 58, 59, 60, 62,
    63, 65, 67, 69, 70, 71, 92, 94,
    107, 109, 115
    Mujib's six-point policy statement,
    33, 36, 45, 46
Ayub Khan, Muhammad, 32, 36, 37,
    40, 43, 44, 74, 82, 104, 114
Ayubnagar, 104(photo)
Azad, Abdus Samad, 50, 55, 107
Azam, Shafiul, 61
Azizur Rahman, Shah, 50, 65–66, 67,
    111

Bakerganj District, 76
BAKSAL. *See* Bangladesh Krishak
    Sramik Awami League
Baluchistan, 26, 30, 37, 40
Bang (tribe), 11
Bangabandhu (Mujibur Rahman), 57
Bangladesh Biman, 29
Bangladesh Krishak Sramik Awami
    League (Bangladesh Peasants,
    Workers, and Peoples League;
    BAKSAL), 50, 57, 58, 59, 65
Bangladesh Muslim League, 65
Bangladesh Nationalist Party (BNP),
    50, 65–67, 70, 71, 92, 115
Bangladesh Observer, 94
Bangladesh Times, 94
Barisal District, 6, 76
Bashar, M. K., 61
"Basic democrats," 43, 44
Battle of Plassey (1757), 13, 16, 17
Bay of Bengal, 6, 11, 98, 100, 106
Bengal, 1, 7–8, 11–28, 30, 35, 37, 70,
    115. *See also* East Bengal; West
    Bengal
Bengal Civil Service, 33

Bengali
  language, 9, 14, 30–31, 41, 42, 49,
    53, 56, 74, 113
  literature, 9–10
  Muslims. *See* Muslims; Vernacular
    elite
  people, 1, 6–7, 8, 18–20, 31, 32, 33,
    36, 37, 53, 70
Bhashani, Maulana Abdul Hamid
    Khan, 41, 43, 57
Bhutto, Zulfiqar Ali Khan, 44, 46, 49,
    51, 98, 101, 102
Bihar, 8, 11, 12, 13, 14, 17, 24, 25, 30,
    36, 53
Black Hole (of Calcutta), 16
BNP. *See* Bangladesh Nationalist Party
Bogra, Muhammad Ali, 32, 39–40, 42,
    43
Bogra District, 4, 12, 64, 76, 77
Bombay, 15, 17, 21, 24, 25, 34
Brahmaputra River, 1, 2, 86, 101
Britain. *See* Great Britain
British Indian Army, 33
British Indian Empire, 103
Britons, 32
Buddhists, 9, 11–13, 69
Burma, 35
  border with, 3, 9, 99, 100, 103

Calcutta, 12, 15, 16, 17, 18, 21–22,
    24–25, 27, 29, 34, 37, 75, 93
Cancun conference (1981), 111
Carey, William, 9
Carter, Jimmy, 107
Castes, 6, 7, 31, 92
Chakma (tribe), 9, 69
Chalna, 6, 103
Chandpur, 12
Chandragupta (ca. 321–296 B.C.), 12
Chandranagar, 15
Chatterjee, Bankim Chandra, 9
Chaudhury, Abul Fazal Muhammad
    Ahsanuddin, 50, 68
Chaudhury, Abu Sayeed, 50, 51, 52,
    105
Chaudhury, Badruddoza, 66
Chaudhury, Hamidul Haq, 94
China. *See* People's Republic of China
Chinsura, 15
Chittagong, 2, 6, 15, 22, 51, 53, 66,
    76, 77, 83, 103, 108
  district, 4, 6, 76, 90, 92
  Hill Tracts, 2, 4, 9, 52, 69, 76, 77,
    99
Cholera Research Laboratory, 90
Christians, 8–9, 93, 105
Civil rights, 45, 50, 52, 53
  limitations on, 50, 57, 58, 60
  political activity, 42, 43, 44
Civil servants, 61, 75
  from outside Bangladesh, 14, 49
Civil Service, 73–76

Civil war, 1, 46, 82, 86, 106
Climate, 6
Clive, Robert, 15–16, 17
CMLA. *See* Military, chief martial law
    administrator
Coal, 4
Colonial enclaves, 15
Combined Opposition Parties, 44
Comilla District, 12, 76, 77, 86, 90
Commonwealth, 52, 98, 106, 110
Communal identity, 24, 27
Communications, 86
Communist Party of Bangladesh, 108
Congress Party. *See* Indian National
    Congress
Connally, John, 107
Constituent Assembly, 29, 31, 39–40,
    41, 42, 45, 62
Constitution (Bangladesh), 50, 52–53,
    55, 57, 62, 67, 68, 109, 114
Cooch Behar, 20
Cornwallis, Marquess, 18–19, 34, 80
Corruption, 55, 57, 61, 63, 68, 69, 75
Cotton, 36, 84, 85
Council Muslim League, 44
Courts. *See* Civil Rights; Government
    of Bangladesh, judiciary
Crops, 79–83, 89
  minor, 3–4, 84, 86
  See also Cotton; Jute; Rice
CSP. *See* Pakistan, Civil Service of
    Pakistan
Culture, 93–94, 110. *See also* Bengali;
    Urdu
Currency. *See* Fiscal policy, internal
Curzon, Marquess of, 24
Cycle-rickshaw, 54(photo)

Dacca, 21. *See also* Dhaka
"Decade of Progress," 36, 44
Defense, 41, 45
Delhi, 13, 15, 17, 19, 27
Democracy, 52
  suspension of, 53, 58, 68. *See also*
    Military, martial law
Democratic League, 62–63
Demographics, 2, 6–9, 79–80, 90, 92
Desai, Morarji, 60
Detainees, 55, 102
Dhaka, 2, 6, 13–14, 15, 18(photo), 22,
    23(photo), 24, 25, 29, 31, 42, 43,
    46, 49, 52, 54(photo), 64, 66, 75,
    76, 77, 83, 90, 98, 102, 107
  Central Jail, 58, 59
  Islamic summit meeting (1973),
    104(photo)
Dhaka District, 13, 76, 92
Diet, 3
  protein, 84
Dinajpur District, 7, 76
Diwani, 17, 19
"Doctrine of Necessity," 40

Dravidians, 6, 11
Dyarchy, 24–25

East African Indians, 35
East Bengal (now Bangladesh), 21, 29,
    30, 31, 32, 34, 35, 36, 40, 41, 42,
    113
    Province (1905), 24, 28, 99
East India Company, 19
Economic development
    East versus West Pakistan, 49
    funds for, 30, 87, 108–110. See also
        Foreign assistance
    lenders' influence, 83
    nineteen-point program, 63, 114, 115
    planning, 74, 107, 114
Economy, 30, 38, 44, 69, 70, 79–87,
    89. See also Fiscal policy, internal
    balance of trade, 87
    denationalization, 85
    nationalization, 56, 57, 84
    price incentives (fixed prices), 83
    private versus public sector, 84, 85
    settlement of debts and assets, 102
Education, 8, 70, 110
    madrassas, 89
    rural primary level, 74, 88–89, 92
    university level, 21, 56, 74, 89, 108
Egypt, 105–106
Elections
    in Bangladesh, 50, 52, 57, 58, 60,
        62, 63, 64–65, 66, 67, 69, 70, 113
    in Pakistan, 40, 41, 42, 43, 44, 45,
        46
Electricity, 4, 85, 86, 101
Elizabeth II (queen of England), 70,
    110
Emigration from Bangladesh, 56, 93,
    100
English language, 9, 30–31, 56, 74
Ershad, Husain Muhammad, 50, 61,
    66, 67, 68–69, 70–71, 77, 83, 85,
    104, 106, 107, 109, 110, 114
Exports, 36, 49, 86, 105. See also
    Foreign exchange; Trade

Family planning, 88, 89, 90, 108
Famine, 43
Faraizi movement, 8
Farakka Barrage, 2, 3, 37, 99, 101, 111
Faridpur District, 7, 8, 76
Farmers Peoples Party. See Krishak
    Praja Party
Fazlul Huq, A. K., 25, 26, 27, 29, 33,
    41, 42, 44, 57, 58, 60, 104, 115
Fazlul Huq "Moni," Sheikh, 55
Federal Court, 40
Fertilizers, 4, 82–83
First War of Independence, 19
Fiscal policy, internal, 41, 45
Fish, 84, 86

Flooding. See Rivers, annual flooding
    by
Foreign assistance, 77–78, 83–84, 87,
    88, 89, 90, 98, 104–111, 116. See
    also Economic development, funds
    for
Foreign exchange, 36, 45, 77, 84, 85
Foreign markets, 36, 85, 86, 105
Foreign policy, 42–43, 45, 55, 109
Foreign relations, 97–111
Fort William, 15
France, 78, 98
Franchise. See Voting qualifications
Frontier, The, 19, 26, 27, 31, 33, 37
Fundamental rights of citizens. See
    Civil rights

Gama, Vasco da, 15
Gandhi (film), 28
Gandhi, Indira, 58, 61, 99, 101, 107
Gandhi, Mohandas Karamchand
    "Mahatma," 6, 25, 28
Ganga-Brahmaputra river system, 86,
    101
Ganga-Kobadak irrigation system, 3,
    37
Ganges River, 1, 2, 3, 6, 11, 19, 37,
    101. See also Padma
Garos (tribe), 9
Gas. See Natural gas
GDP. See Gross domestic product
George V (king of England), 24
Ghulam Muhammad, 32, 39–40, 42
Gopala (750 A.D.), 12
Gopalganj Subdivision, 7
Government of Bangladesh
    administrative units, 76
    civil administration, 56, 73–76
    civil service. See Civil servants;
        Civil service
    constitution. See Constitution, of
        Bangladesh
    elections. See Elections, in
        Bangladesh
    in exile, 50, 51
    goals, 3, 79, 114
    gram sarkars (village governments),
        69
    judiciary, 52, 57, 62
    martial law. See Military, martial
        law
    ministry of home affairs, 60, 62
    Mujibism (or Mujibbad), 52
    organization, 60, 62, 76
    parliament, 50, 52, 55, 58, 63, 65,
        68, 83, 104(photo)
    provisional, 50, 51
    See also Foreign policy; Military,
        martial law
Government of India Act of 1909
    (Morley-Minto Act), 22

Government of India Act of 1919
    (Montagu-Chelmsford Act), 24, 73
Government of India Act of 1935, 25,
    39, 40, 73
Great Bengal Famine of 1943–1944, 43
Great Britain, 77, 98, 106, 110
    political parties, 20, 27
    rule by, 1, 7, 12, 15–16, 17–28, 73,
        76, 103
    See also Commonwealth
Great Calcutta Killing, 27
Gross domestic product (GDP), 44, 84
Group of 77, 111
Gujarati, 30
Gupta Empire, 12

Handicrafts, 21
Haq, Ziaul, 98
Hardinge Bridge, 37
Harijans, 6
Harsha empire, 12
Hasina Wajid, 67
Hastings, Warren, 17
Health, 87, 90, 92, 108
Hindi, 30
Hindus, 1, 6–7, 8, 11–13, 14, 15, 30,
    32, 33, 34, 38, 69, 92–93, 100,
    102, 115
    in government, 52
    Marathas, 15, 19
    money lenders, 16
    non-Congress, 26
    political separation from Muslims,
        17, 19, 22–25
    reformists, 9, 18, 20
Home rule, 20
Hooghly, 15
Huda, Mirza Nurul, 62, 67, 68
Huq, A. K. Fazlul. See Fazlul Huq, A.
    K.
Huq, Muhammad Shamsul, 62
Husain, Kamal, 55, 67
Hydroelectric plant, 4, 69

ICS. See Indian Civil Service
IDA. See International Development
    Association
IDBP. See Industrial Development
    Bank of Pakistan
IMET. See Military, International
    Military Education and Training
IMF. See International Monetary Fund
Imports, 3, 21, 83–84, 105
Independence, 1, 28, 29, 43, 46, 49,
    114, 115
India
    alliance with Bangladesh, 51, 55, 57,
        58, 60–61, 78, 100, 109
    border with Bangladesh, 3, 9, 70,
        99, 100
    intervention by, 1, 46, 51, 97, 98

migration of Bangladeshis into, 93,
    100
partition of (1947), 1, 7, 14, 17, 26,
    27, 28, 35, 99
recognition of Bangladesh by, 49,
    51, 98
relations with Pakistan and
    Bangladesh, 41, 44, 58, 101, 110
water negotiations with Bangladesh,
    2–3, 37, 99, 101, 111
India Councils Act of 1861, 21
India Councils Act of 1892
    (Lansdowne Act), 21, 22
India Independence Act of 1947, 39
Indian Civil Service (ICS), 32, 33
Indian National Congress, 22, 24, 25,
    26, 27
Indo-Aryans, 6, 11
Indus basin development, 36
Industrial Development Bank of
    Pakistan (IDBP), 37
Inheritance patterns, 80, 82
International basket case, 53
International Development Association
    (IDA), 110–111
International Monetary Fund (IMF),
    87, 110
International Rice Research Institute,
    82
Irrigation, 37, 80, 82–83
Islam, 7–8, 13–15, 105, 113. See also
    Mughal rule; Muslims
Islam, Aminul. See Aminul Islam
Islam, Syed Nazrul. See Nazrul Islam,
    Syed
Islamabad, 49, 102
Islamic Conference, 29, 105
Islamic Democratic League, 65
Islamic state, 11, 42, 45, 71, 104
    versus secular government, 7, 38–39
Islamic states, 98, 103–106
Ispahani (family), 34–35
Ittefaq (newspaper), 57, 94

Jafar, Mir. See Mir Jafar
Jamalpur District, 76
Jamuna, 2. See also Brahmaputra River
Janata Party, 60, 101
Japan, 64, 98, 106, 109–110
Jasimuddin, 93
Jatiyo Ganatantrik Dal (National
    Democratic Party; JAGODAL), 64,
    65, 71
Jatiyo Rakhi Bahini (Security Force),
    56, 58, 77
Jatiyo Samajtantrik Party (National
    Socialist Party; JSD), 56, 57, 59,
    60, 61, 64, 70, 77
Jessore District, 7, 76, 77, 81(photo)
Jews, 105
Jinnah, Fatima, 44

Jinnah, Muhammad Ali, 24, 25, 26, 27, 29, 30–32, 34, 38, 39, 44, 115
Joint electorates, 25, 38, 52. *See also* Separate electorates
JSD. *See* Jatiyo Samajtantrik Party
Jute, 3, 18, 21, 34, 35, 36, 84, 85, 86

Kampuchea, 109
Kamruzzaman, A.H.M., 59
Kaptai, 4
Karachi, 29, 31, 34, 35, 40, 42, 43
Kashmir, 26, 44
Khalid Musharaf. *See* Musharaf, Khalid
Khan, Abdul Monem. *See* Monem Khan, Abdul
Khan, Agha Muhammad Yahya. *See* Yahya Khan, Agha Muhammad
Khan, A. K., 35, 43
Khan, Ataur Rahman. *See* Ataur Rahman Khan
Khan, A.Z.M. Obaidullah. *See* Obaidullah Khan, A.Z.M.
Khan, M. H., 62
Khan, Muhammad Ayub. *See* Ayub Khan, Muhammad
Khan, Nawabzada Liaqat Ali. *See* Liaqat Ali Khan, Nawabzada
Khan, Sir Syed Ahmad. *See* Ahmad Khan, Sir Syed
Khojas, 34
Khomeini, Ayatollah Ruhollah, 105, 115
Khulna District, 2, 6, 7, 37, 76, 83, 90, 92, 103
Kissinger, Henry, 55, 98, 107
KPP. *See* Krishak Praja Party
Krishak Praja Party (KPP), 26, 41
Krishak Sramik Party (KSP), 41, 42, 57
KSP. *See* Krishak Sramik Party
Kulinism, 13
Kushtia District, 76

Labor
   disputes, 36, 42
   emigration of workers, 85, 86, 93, 105
Lahore, 26, 38, 45
   Islamic summit meeting (1974), 98, 102, 103
   See also "Pakistan Resolution"
Land, 2, 34, 79–80, 82
   reform bill, 14, 41
Landlords. *See* Zamindars
Language. *See* Bengali; Urdu
Lansdowne, Marquess of, 21
Lansdowne Act. *See* India Councils Act of 1892
Law-and-order problems, 53, 57, 60, 69
Law of the Sea Conference, 100–101
League, The. *See* Muslim League

Leftists, 55, 58, 59, 65, 70, 106, 115
Legal due process, 53
Liaqat Ali Khan, Nawabzada, 31–32, 39
Libya, 60, 105–106
Linlithgow, Marquess of, 27
Literacy, 88. *See also* Education
Lucknow, 24, 26

Macdonald, Ramsay, 25
Madras, 16, 17, 19, 21
Madrassas, 89
Maghs (tribe), 9
Mahabharata, 12
Mahmud, A. G., 61, 64, 69
Mahmud of Ghazni (1001 A.D.), 13
Malaria, 90
Mansur Ali, 59
Manzur, Muhammad, 66
Martyrs' monument, 31
Marwaris, 22, 34
Mashiur Rahman, 65, 66
Mauryan Empire, 12
Medicine, 8. *See also* Health
Meerut, 19
Middle East, 85, 105–106, 107
Military
   academy at Comilla, 77
   air force, 77
   Ansars, 78
   Bangladesh Army, 53, 64, 77. *See also* Mukti Bahini
   Bangladesh Police, 78
   Bangladesh Rifles, 78
   chief martial law administrator (CMLA), 50, 59, 60, 63, 68
   East Pakistan Police, 78
   East Pakistan Rifles, 78
   equipment, 77–78
   freedom fighters and returnees, 55–56, 77
   International Military Education and Training (IMET), 108
   lack of Bengalis in, 19–20, 30, 33, 38, 49
   martial and nonmartial races, 19, 33
   martial law, 43, 44, 60–61, 68–71, 83, 94, 113, 114
   militia, 45
   navy, 77
   Pakistan Army, 32, 33, 56, 60
   "people's army," 56, 59, 77
   personnel, 14, 33, 55
   rebellion against central power, 73
   and Soviet Union, 77–78, 109
   and United States, 78, 108
Minto, 4th Earl of, 22
Mir Jafar, 16, 17, 32
Mirza, Iskander, 32, 40, 42, 43
Mizos (tribe), 99
Mofussil (hinterland), 17
Monem Khan, Abdul, 43

Montagu-Chelmsford Act. *See*
    Government of India Act of 1919
Morley, Viscount, 22
Morley-Minto Act. *See* Government of
    India Act of 1909
Mountbatten, Earl, 27
Mughal rule, 7, 14–15, 17–19, 73
Muhajirs (refugees), 31
Muhammad (Prophet), 7
Muhammad, Ghulam. *See* Ghulam
    Muhammad
Muhammad Ali, Chaudhury, 32, 42
Muhammad Ali Bogra. *See* Bogra,
    Muhammad Ali
Muhammadan Anglo-Oriental College,
    22
Muhammadullah, 50, 68
Muhith, A.M.A., 69, 83, 111
Mujib. *See* Mujibur Rahman, Sheikh
Mujibnagar, 51
Mujibur Rahman, Sheikh
    assassination, 58–60, 64, 103
    and India, 99, 100
    and military, 55–56, 61, 75, 77
    and Pakistan, 98, 102
    political arrest, 42, 44
    political philosophy, 7, 55–56, 65,
        84, 85, 93, 103, 115
    regime, 9, 44, 49–58, 74, 76, 82, 92,
        94, 106
    six points, 33, 36, 45, 46
    and Suhrawardy, 41, 44
    and superpowers, 106–108
    and Ziaur Rahman, 51
Mukti Bahini (rebel force), 46, 51, 53,
    65
Murshidabad, 14, 16, 17
Musharaf, Khalid, 50, 59
Mushtaque Ahmad, Khondakar, 50, 51,
    55, 58–59, 60, 62–63, 68, 76, 98,
    103, 104, 114
Muslim League, 14, 18–19, 22,
    23(photo), 24, 25, 26, 27, 29, 31,
    32, 35, 38–39, 40, 41, 42, 43–44,
    52, 57, 70, 115
Muslims, 1, 6–9, 11, 13–15, 19, 30, 32,
    33, 74, 88, 89, 93, 100, 102, 103,
    104
    business and land owners, 34
    Islamic fundamentalists, 93, 104–105,
        115
    Ismaili (Aga Khani) branch of
        Shi'ism, 7, 22, 34
    Ithna Ashari Shi'a, 7, 14
    Khojas, 34
    middle class, 18
    nationally oriented elite, 17, 25, 27,
        29, 31. *See also* Urdu elite
    political separation from Hindus, 17,
        19, 22–25, 26
    Sunnis, 7, 14
    vernacular elite, 17, 25
Muslim state or states, 27, 39

Mustafizur Rahman, 9
Mutiny, 19, 64, 77
Mymensingh District, 9, 76

Nadia District, 13, 76
Narayanganj, 2, 35, 42, 85
National Assembly. *See* Pakistan,
    parliament
National Awami Party, 43
    "pro-Moscow" faction, 57, 108
    "pro-Peking" faction, 57, 65
National Democratic Front, 44
National Democratic Party. *See* Jatiyo
    Ganatantrik Dal
Nationalist Front, 64–65
National identity (India), 24
National security council, 68
National Socialist Party. *See* Jatiyo
    Samajtantrik Party
Natural gas, 4, 82, 86, 100–101, 110
Nawab-nazim (title), 17
Nawab of Dhaka, 22, 23(photo), 25
Nazimuddin, Khwaja Sir, 25, 27, 29,
    31, 32, 39–40, 44
Nazrul Islam, Syed, 51, 59
Nehru, Jawaharlal, 24
Nehru, Motilal, 24
Nepal, 2, 101, 103
New Delhi, 12, 25, 59, 100, 102
Nixon, Richard M., 55, 98, 107
Noakhali, 76, 85
Nonaligned movement, 111
Northwest Frontier. *See* Frontier, The
Nurul Amin, 31, 42, 44

Obaidullah Khan, A.Z.M., 69, 101
Organization of the Islamic
    Conference. *See* Islamic
    Conference
Orissa, 14, 17, 24, 25
Osmany, Muhammad Abdul Ghani,
    51, 65, 67

Pabna District, 76
Padma, 2, 4. *See also* Ganges River
Pakistan
    administrative systems and
        Bangladesh, 73
    autonomy of various parts, 39, 41,
        45, 49
    Civil Service of Pakistan (CSP), 32–
        33, 55, 74
    concept of, 26–27
    Constitution, 31, 37–39, 40, 42, 43,
        45, 46
    East Pakistan (now Bangladesh), 6,
        8, 11, 12, 20, 26, 29, 30, 33, 36,
        37, 38, 39, 43, 44, 46, 49, 51, 52,
        55, 74, 97, 100, 113
    Foreign Service, 51, 74
    governmental positions in, 39–40,
        41, 42, 43, 44

judiciary, 45
parliament, 40, 42, 43, 44, 52
Peoples Party, 46
Police Service of, 74
residual (1971–), 7, 36, 52, 55, 85,
    98, 101, 102, 107, 109, 110. *See
    also* Pakistan, West Pakistan
united (1947–1971), 9–10, 14, 28,
    29–46, 56, 57, 62, 97, 98, 99, 102,
    106
West Pakistan (now residual
    Pakistan), 8, 11, 20, 30, 31, 32,
    34, 38, 39, 41, 42, 44, 45, 49, 51,
    53, 55, 56, 61, 74, 75, 85, 115
See also Military, martial law
Pakistan Industrial and Commercial
    Investment Corporation (PICIC),
    37
Pakistan International Airlines (PIA),
    29
Pakistan Observer, 94
"Pakistan Resolution," 26, 39
Pala Dynasty, 12–13
Pali, 9
"Parity" formulas for representation,
    38, 42
Pathan, 20
Patuakhali District, 6, 76
Peace Corps, 110
Peasants and Workers Party. *See*
    Krishak Sramik Party
People (newspaper), 94
People's Republic of Bangladesh, 1
People's Republic of China, 97, 98,
    102, 106, 109, 110
Permanent Settlement of Bengal, 18
Persian, 34, 74
PIA. *See* Pakistan International
    Airlines
PICIC. *See* Pakistan Industrial and
    Commercial Investment
    Corporation
Police, 74, 75, 77–78
Political chronology of Bangladesh, 50
Political freedom, limited, 42, 43, 44,
    49, 69
Population, 1
    annual growth rate, 2, 84, 87–88,
        92, 113
    density, 2
    land per capita, 2, 79–80, 82
    planning, 63, 87
    See also Demographics
Ports. *See* Seaports
PRC. *See* People's Republic of China
Prisoners
    political, 57, 69
    of war, 55, 101, 102
Protein production, 84
Pundra (Pundravardhana), 12
Punjab, The, 11, 19–20, 24, 26, 27, 30,
    32, 34, 36, 37, 38, 82
    Mussalmans, 33

Purdah, 89
Pushtu, 30

Quran, 8

Rahman, Mashiur. *See* Mashiur
    Rahman
Rahman, Mustafizur. *See* Mustafizur
    Rahman
Rahman, Shah Azizur. *See* Azizur
    Rahman, Shah
Rahman, Sheikh Mujibur. *See* Mujibur
    Rahman, Sheikh
Rahman, Ziaur. *See* Ziaur Rahman
Rajasthan, 22, 34
Rajshahi District, 76
Rakhi Bahini. *See* Jatiyo Rakhi Bahini
Rangpur District, 76
Reagan, Ronald, 107
Refugees, 31, 32, 36, 38–39, 53, 74,
    102
Religion, 92–93. *See also* Buddhists;
    Christians; Hindus; Muslims;
    Sikhs
Repatriates, 55, 56, 61
Representation, 45, 49
Revolution, 115
Rice, 3, 4(photo), 36, 79, 81(photo),
    82–84
Rightists, 55, 65
Ripon, Marquess of, 20
Rivers, 5(photo)
    annual flooding, by, 3, 82
    Damodar, 1
    Hooghly, 15, 22, 37
    Indus, 11
    Karnaphuli, 1, 4, 69
    Meghna, 1, 2
    Pusar, 6
    Tista, 2
    transportation on, 4
    See also Brahmaputra River; Ganges
    River
Round Table Conferences, 25
Roy, Raja Ram Mohan, 9, 20

Salinity, 3, 37
Samatata, Kingdom of, 12
Sanskrit, 9, 12, 30
Santhals (tribe), 9
SARC. *See* South Asian Regional
    Cooperation
Sarkar, Abu Husain, 42
Sati, 20
Sattar, Abdus, 50, 62, 63, 64, 65, 66,
    67, 68
Sayem, A.S.M., 50, 59, 60, 61, 62, 63
Scheduled Castes, 6, 31, 92
Seaports, 2, 6, 12, 22, 53, 103, 108
SEATO. *See* Southeast Asia Treaty
    Organization

Secularism, 7, 52, 105. *See also* Islamic
    state, versus secular government
Senas, 13
Separate electorates, 22, 24, 25, 38,
    41, 52. *See also* Joint electorates
Sepoys, 19, 59
Serampore, 15
Shahabuddin, Khwaja, 31, 43
Shahid Minar, 31
Shahjahan (emperor), 15
Sharia, 8
Shariatullah of Faridpur, 8
Sher-i-Bangla Nagar, 104(photo)
Siddiqi, Kader, 60
Sikhs, 22, 30, 32, 34
Simla, 22
Simon, Viscount, 25
Sind, 13, 24, 25, 26, 27, 30, 34, 37
Single-issue politics, 66
Sirajuddaula, 15–17, 32
Socialism, 52, 56, 57, 84, 85, 115
South Asian Regional Cooperation
    (SARC), 86–87, 97, 102–103
Southeast Asia Treaty Organization
    (SEATO), 90
Soviet Union, 57, 59, 71, 77, 78, 102,
    105, 106–109
Srirampur, 15
Suez crisis, 43
Sufism, 8, 9
Suhrawardy, Husain Shaheed, 27, 29,
    39, 41, 42, 44, 58, 115
Syeds, 7
Sylhet District, 2, 6, 9, 28, 76, 86

Tagore, Sir Rabindranath, 9–10, 30, 93
Taher, Abu, 59–60, 70
Tangail District, 76
Tashkent, agreement at, 44, 45
Tawab, M. G., 61
Taxation. *See* Fiscal policy, internal
Textiles, 21, 35, 36, 84, 85
Thana, 76
Timber, 69, 70
Tippera District. *See* Comilla District
Tipu Sultan, 19
Trade, 30, 36, 41, 45, 56, 86–87, 102,
    109–110
Trading companies, European, 15
Transportation, 6, 86. *See also* Rivers,
    transportation on
Treaty of Friendship, Cooperation, and
    Peace (1972), 99
Tribes in tracts, 4
Tripuras (tribe), 9
Twenty-one points (United Front), 41,
    42, 45

United Front, 41, 42, 45
United Kingdom. *See* Great Britain

United Nations, 88, 97–99, 102, 106,
    109, 110–111
United States, 78, 88, 102–110
United States Information Service
    (USIS), 106–107, 108
Untouchables, 6
Urbanization. *See* Demographics
Urdu, 7, 8, 14, 30–31, 34, 36, 42
Urdu elite, 25, 29, 32, 33, 40, 41, 43,
    44, 74. *See also* Muslims,
    nationally oriented elite
USIS. *See* United States Information
    Service
Uttar Pradesh, 2, 12, 19, 30

Vanga, 1, 11, 12
Vernacular elite, 7, 41, 58, 74
Victoria (queen of England), 20
Vietnam, 109
Vikramapur, 13
"Voice of Independent Bangladesh," 51
Voting qualifications, 21, 40

Wajid, Hasina. *See* Hasina Wajid
Water
    drinking, 90, 91(photo)
    rights, 99, 101, 111
Wavell, Viscount, 27
Weaving, 21
Wellesley, Arthur (Duke of
    Wellington), 19
Wellesley, Marquess of, 19
Wellington, Duke of, 19
West Bengal (now part of India), 1, 2,
    7, 12, 13, 35, 74, 93, 100
West Germany, 98
Women
    family planning, 88, 89
    indirect election of, 45, 52, 57
    purdah, 89
World Bank, 61, 106, 110

Yahya Khan, Agha Muhammad, 33,
    44, 45, 46, 49, 62

Zamindars, 14, 18–19
Zia. *See* Ziaur Rahman
Ziaur Rahman
    assassination, 66–67
    and chief of staff position, 51, 59
    and foreign governments, 97, 98,
        100, 101, 102, 103, 106, 107, 109,
        110
    and military, 61–62, 68, 77
    and Mujib, 51, 93
    nineteen-point program, 63, 114, 115
    political philosophy, 60, 69, 71, 74,
        75, 93, 104, 113, 115
    regime, 60–66, 75–76, 82, 83, 84,
        85, 86, 92, 103, 105